W9-APC-893

A Little Greatness

Joe Noland

ⒸrestBooks

Salvation Army National Publications
615 Slaters Lane
Alexandria, Virginia 22313

Endorsement

Joe Noland's *A Little Greatness*, with its warmth and wit, its color and clarity, delights the heart, stimulates the mind and nourishes the soul. The writing redefines greatness, countering the secular myth that greatness is reserved for a select few. Noland puts greatness in the perspective of our relationship with God and our enablement by the Holy Spirit whom he describes as "our stealth missile, gentle guide and friendly facilitator."

The author's daring creativity and skilled wordplay jars the reader awake by his pyrotechnical phrasing, garnished prose and non-traditional format—all adding dazzle and pizzazz to the text. Pointed truths explode from his oxymorons, e.g., "discordant harmony, gentle boldness, lowered to new heights, brilliant shadows, defiant obedience, Saul's blindsight." His hallmark of humor scintillates throughout. Read what he does with the fact that he was born in Mercy Hospital and his wife born in Grace Hospital.

Heart-hitting stories call us back to life's core values and commitments. Scripture is deftly woven into the fabric of each page and the 26-week Bible Study and Discussion Guide at the end of the book provides a practical dimension for either independent or group study.

A mini autobiography interspersed throughout the text adds color and character to the work. Life lessons emerge from such events as his playground confrontation with the school bully, boyhood attachment to a giant oak, timidity in buttonhole witnessing as a cadet and even how his ill-tempered cat became a "purr-fect example of great grace."

For those of us who have known Joe Noland over the years, his accomplishments have been legendary. Who can forget the spectacular program he imagineered at The Salvation Army's 1985 International Youth Congress? Or the musicals written and produced for territorial congresses? Or opening of the work in Micronesia, marking the Army's commencement in its 100th country? Now that same energetic daring and creativity has been invested in bringing readers *A Little Greatness*. This adventure in reading offers exciting insights and inspiration for all who aspire to live above mediocrity, in response to Christ's call to true greatness.

Colonel Henry Gariepy (R)

Copyright © 1998 The Salvation Army

Published by Crest Books, Salvation Army National Publications
615 Slaters Lane, Alexandria, VA 22313
(703) 684-5500 • Fax: (703) 684-5539
http://publications.salvationarmyusa.org

Printed in the United States of America

All rights reserved. No part of this publication may be reproduced, stored
in a retrieval system, or transmitted in any form or by any means—
electronic, mechanical, photocopy, recording—without the prior written permission of the publisher. The only exception is brief quotations
in printed reviews.

Unless otherwise noted, Scripture taken from the New King James Version. Copyright © 1979, 1980, 1982 by Thomas Nelson, Inc. Used by
permission. All rights reserved.

Scripture noted NIV taken from the Holy Bible, New International
Version. Copyright © 1973, 1978, 1984 by International Bible Society.

Layout and design by Timothy Clark.
Cover design by Henry Cao and Timothy Clark

Library of Congress Catalog Card Number: 98-73190

ISBN: 0-9657601-4-6

Dedicated to Doris, the most creative person I know. Her inspiration and example have not only contributed to the flow, they have also taught me the true meaning of *a little greatness*.

Contents

Acknowledgments

The inspiration for this manuscript came when we were living in Hawaii and I was recuperating from serious surgery. I simply put pen to paper and the words started to flow. I want to pay tribute to those who significantly contributed to the flow.

First to my physician, Dr. Dennis Myer, one of the most positive people I have ever known. I refer to him in one of the chapters. The diagnosis of a potentially life-threatening ailment begins a roller coaster ride that is unfathomable to the uninitiated. May you never have to take this ride. But if you do, I pray that you will have a physician who jumps in the car and takes the highs and lows right alongside you. He never doubted. He always encouraged. He constantly reminded me that a positive mental attitude was life transforming. He was always reassuring in his assessment that, "God isn't finished with you yet." He chastised kindly and gently by not letting me forget that the

Great Physician was also in the coaster alongside me. After each session with the good doctor I felt a tremendous surge of creative energy and release. Thank you Dr. Myer for contributing to the flow.

Second to Jenny Ing and Ken Harding. Jenny was my secretary at the time. She took my scribbled notes and miraculously transformed them into legible pages. Without ever complaining she untiringly and efficiently coped with revision after revision. The "aloha" spirit is not a figment of the imagination. It really does exist in Hawaii; Jenny Ing is the consummate example of that spirit. Ken was my advisory board chairman and very experienced as a professional editor. His advice, counsel and editing made this a much easier and palatable experience. Thank you Ken and Jenny for contributing to the flow.

Third, I must pay tribute to our children: Rob, Denise and Guy. The experiences of Rob and Guy are peppered throughout these pages. Denise came into our life in Hawaii through the good graces of Rob. And I must say that he has excellent taste. She has already been included in the next manuscript. This book would have been impossible without them. They are my inspiration and my life. Their energy and lust for life fuel my creativity. They keep me young. Thank you, kids, for contributing to the flow.

And finally, I must acknowledge the work and inspiration of the Holy Spirit in my life and in the life of this book. The following prayer has been echoed continuously throughout this creative process:

Spirit of the living God,
    Fall afresh on me.
Spirit of the living God,
    Fall afresh on me.
Break me, melt me, mold me, fill me;
        Spirit of the living God,
Fall afresh on me.

Thank you, Lord, for creating the flow.

Prologue

I have labored under the illusion that greatness is reserved for that select few endowed with a fortuitous combination of luck, talent and intelligence.

The child prodigy
  The Nobel Peace Prize winner
The world class athlete
  The Olympic medal winner
The Rhodes scholar
  The Forbes 100 choice
The West Point valedictorian
  The Medal of Honor winner
The Broadway actor
  The Tony Award winner

Greatness seems somehow connected with being at the center of attention, either through self-promotion or hero-worship. A world heavyweight asserted defiantly, "I am the greatest!" A record-setting hockey player was being anointed "The Great One"!

"Meanwhile," I reasoned, "the rest of us will, at best, become great-grandparents sitting meekly on the sidelines, consigned, we assume, to a life that is meager, mediocre and miserable."

But as I grew spiritually, I discovered that greatness is actually the opposite of what we think. We have been deceived and misled because *the prince of darkness* has twisted and distorted the true meaning of greatness. Getting a proper perspective involves shifting our perspective to learn about the greatness of God rather than the greatness of man.

Greatness, I would come to appreciate in later years, is a gift that flows directly from God's infinite wisdom, generosity and love. More than that, it is a state of being present, of being *with* God.

Comparative greatness—that is, judging worth by the ability to perform better than others—as we usually think of it, is not the route to spiritual greatness—indeed, it is the opposite! True greatness, based on the love of God, is the *shared* greatness found in compassion, rather than competition; in humility, rather than hubris.

Was our Lord great, as defined by worldly standards? Absolutely not! Did He win any prizes, polls or popularity contests? Of course not! Did the Roman government decorate Him with a medal? No way! Did the religious hierarchy appoint Him to their high council? Hardly!

If you were seeking mortal greatness, you would not travel the path Jesus trod. If you were seeking earthly greatness, you would not run the course Jesus ran. If you were seeking greatness through human achievment, you would not climb the mountain Jesus scaled.

For on that mountain Jesus taught a different kind of greatness. On that mountain He delivered a sermon that boldly contradicts man's conceit about greatness. On that mountain He defined greatness in terms of riches in heaven rather than treasures on earth (Matthew 5-7).

The key to greatness, He proclaimed, lies in just *how,* and *how well,* we treat others, even our most vicious enemy, or our worst nightmare, or even someone meaningless to us.

> "... *whatever you want men to do to you, do also to them* ..." (Matthew 7:12).

Thus, Jesus presents us with a Golden Rule for attaining greatness. Whoever follows this rule will understand the true meaning of the Laws of Moses and the lessons of the prophets. They shall know God and "... shall be called great in the Kingdom of Heaven" (Matthew 5:19).

We can't all be world-class athletes like Michael Jordan, but we can all be great in the Kingdom of Heaven. We can't be megastars, but we can all know something of greatness as we experience a little Kingdom of Heaven on earth.

Any of us *can*, but few of us *will*. Jesus practices what He preaches. Are we willing to practice what He preaches? In the stillness of Mount Golgotha, Jesus climbed His final, painful pedestal. He proclaimed, "And he who does not take his cross and follow after Me is not worthy of Me" (Matthew 10:38).

We cry out, "But Lord, the cross is too heavy!" We need not feel overburdened or abandoned, however. Jesus left us, we now know, to fulfill His earlier promise to create a place for us in heaven. But He did not leave us empty-handed. To assist us, we have the power of the Holy Spirit, a Guide, Comforter and Helper who will never leave us.

We often forget about this third person of the Holy Trinity. God the Father we think we know about; God the Son we want to know more about; but God the Holy Ghost we hardly know. And yet, Jesus says, "And I will pray the Father, and He will give you another Helper, that He may abide with you forever" (John 14:16).

Who is this Helper? Our stealth missile, our secret weapon. He is a part of the armament of our salvation. Through the help of the Holy Spirit we can accomplish miracles in our own lives. He enables us to develop greatness and build up our treasure—not on earth, but in Heaven.

Forty days after His death on the cross, Jesus' promise of greatness was confirmed at Pentecost to His followers, who had been scattered throughout the hills and deserts of the Holy Land.

Through the Holy Spirit, Christ's disciples received God's revelation of a revolution that was about to begin. They began to understand the full benefits of great power, the mighty bequest of great grace, and the awesome bounty of great joy. Their insights came from knowing God, and they began to find a little greatness in their lives.

That was then and there. This is here and now, and things have not changed. For us, greatness must still be re-defined and made clear. The Word is our source of information and inspiration. The Holy Spirit is our guide and facilitator.

Like the early disciples, we too can have a Pentecostal experience. The Acts of the Apostles will show us how. As followers of Jesus, we too can know a little greatness in our lives.

To reap this harvest we need only believe with all our hearts.

Part 1

———◆◇◆———

Great Power

And with great power the apostles gave witness to the resurrection of the Lord Jesus (Acts 4:33a).

Spontaneous Spiritual Combustion

Spontaneous spiritual combustion is the greatest power known to man. It was ignited in the Upper Room, and its spontaneous spread has been unstoppable. The power of the throne could not stop it. The power of the Trinity is enduring because it is the source of all power.

The word *power* in Acts 1:8 is translated from the Greek word *dunamis*, which means *explosive power. Dynamite* was named after this word. *Dynamo* is an extension of this discovery, suggesting the spontaneous conversion of energy into great power.

That benign band of believers could not begin to comprehend the enormity of the creative force within them. The energy exerted was not of their own making. The vitality unleashed was not of their own strength. The initiative demonstrated was not motivated by self-will. They were imbued with power from on high.

The Apostle Paul began to grasp the significance of this force when he wrote, "that the God of our Lord Jesus Christ, the Father of glory, may give to you the spirit of wisdom and

revelation in the knowledge of Him, the eyes of your under-
standing being enlightened; that you may know ... what is
the exceeding greatness of His power toward us who believe,
according to the working of His mighty power which He
worked in Christ when He raised Him from the dead and
seated Him at His right hand in the heavenly places ... And
He put all things under His feet, and gave Him to be head
over all things to the church, which is His body, the fullness
of Him who fills all in all" (Ephesians 1:17-20, 22-23).

You can learn something of His greatness. But more important, you too can be filled with the fullness of His *power!*

When the Day of Pentecost had fully come, they were all with one accord in one place. And suddenly there came a sound from heaven, as of a rushing mighty wind, and it filled the whole house where they were sitting. Then there appeared to them divided tongues, as of fire, and one sat upon each of them. And they were all filled with the Holy Spirit and began to speak with other tongues, as the Spirit gave them utterance.

And there were dwelling in Jerusalem Jews, devout men, from every nation under heaven. And when this sound occurred, the multitude came together, and were confused, because everyone heard them speak in his own language. Then they were all amazed and marveled, saying to one another, "Look, are not all these who speak Galileans? And how is it that we hear, each in our own language in which we were born? Parthians and Medes and Elamites, those dwelling in Mesopotamia, Judea and Cappadocia, Pontus and Asia, Phrygia and Pamphylia, Egypt and the parts of Libya adjoining Cyrene, visitors from Rome, both Jews and proselytes, Cretans and Arabs—we hear them speaking in our own tongues the wonderful works of God." So they were all amazed and perplexed, saying to one another, "Whatever could this mean?"

—Acts 2:1-13

One

Discordant Harmony

Symphony concerts, I must confess, often bore me. Don't get me wrong. I have tremendous respect for the music-making process. It takes great skill to blend a hundred discordant musicians into a singular harmonic unit. The challenge of transforming discord into accord is no small matter. I also know that, without discord, we cannot recognize and appreciate harmony. It's just that I'm more of an action-oriented, visually oriented kind of person. That's why "tuning up" and the percussion section are my favorite parts of a symphony concert.

During the tuning process, each player does his own thing. The sound is ear splitting, even glass shattering. But I enjoy it because the contrast between chaos and conformity is so absurd. I am reminded from whence we come and where we might be going. It is life being played out in front of me.

In the beginning, God brought the order of creation out of chaos:

> *In the beginning God created the heavens and the earth. The earth was without form, and void [chaos]; and darkness was on the face of the deep. And the spirit of God was hovering over the face of the waters* (Genesis 1:1-2).

After the flood, God brought order out of chaos. After the cross, God once more brought order out of chaos. And after Pentecost, God again brought order out of chaos.

And the beat goes on!

A symphony was written, orchestrated and assembled in the Upper Room:

> *They were all with one accord in one place* (Acts 2:1b).

The Master's promise was about to be fulfilled and His great power revealed:

> *But you shall receive power when the Holy Spirit has come upon you; and you shall be witnesses to me in Jerusalem, and in all Judea and Samaria, and to the end of the earth* (Acts 1:8).

There was great anticipation in the air.
The masterpiece was mounted.
The players were poised.
The signal was sounded.
The tune-up began. There were ...
Tongues as of fire.
Sound as of wind.
Speech as of wine ...

… as the Spirit gave them utterance (Acts 2:2-4).

Each life must be tuned with the Master's touch to take part in this grand symphony.

And the beat goes on!

The percussion section is where the action is. My eyes and ears are glued to the glue that holds the music together. Dramatic conflict gives substance to the symphonic script. There is great suspense as I sit on the edge of my seat waiting for the triangle to "ping." I am drawn into the conflict between timpani, triangle and timbrel as each competes for its rightful place in the score. And I am ever conscious of the bass drum's subtle beat as it holds the plot together while the conflict is being resolved.

Each life must be timed with the Master's touch.

And the beat goes on!

The Great Musical Revival

Just as there are many parts to our bodies, so it is with Christ's body. We are all parts of it, and it takes every one of us to make it complete, for we each have different work to do. So we belong to each other, and each needs all the others (Romans 12:4-5, Living Bible).

My wife captured this concept in the following parable:

It is said, though the story may not be true, that the instruments gathered together in Music Land for a great musical revival. They came from the east and the west, the north and the south. The trumpets came, the harp and the oboe, the flute, violin, cello and drum. Loud playing instruments, soft-playing instruments—from the tiniest bell to the big brass euphonium—all gathered together for the Great Musical Revival.

As it so often happens in gatherings of this kind, the instruments began to share with one another their wonderful musical aptitudes.

The trumpet declared that he could play with such force and majesty that kings and generals marched to his music. The violin said, in smooth tones, that the music he played could bring tears to your eyes.

The flute, not to be outdone, said that he could play so light and sweet that often he sounded like a bird!

One by one, each instrument extolled its own virtue until finally the piano silenced them all by saying that he alone had the ability to play in seven octaves. "I can play high and I can play low," he said. "I can play fast and I can play slow— and I have much to contribute to the Great Musical Revival." Everyone was very impressed, and agreed that it was so!

The little drum sat sadly in the corner. "I have but one note!" he thought. "I have nothing to offer compared to these instruments." So he left the gathering and hid in a cane field.

The time came when the instruments decided that it was time to begin to play together. But much to their horror, their music was terrible! The trumpets played fast and the violins played slow; the flute played high and the oboe played low! They stopped the racket and checked the music. It seemed to be in order. They checked the tuning of the instruments, and that was fine as well. Suddenly, someone noticed that the drum was not in his place. "We must find him," they cried. Everyone left to find the drum. When they found him, they said, "We need you to play our music!" But the little drum said, "I can't play high, and I can't play low—I have just one note! Not much to contribute to the Great Musical Revival!"

Then the piano said, as only he could, "You are needed, my friend, to set the tempo, to help us keep our music together. Without you our music is quite incomplete!"

And the beat goes on!

We can see in every discordant life a potential for harmony. The great symphony of life began with the Master's touch, and His sanctified stroke has reverberated down through the decades. There was discord at Calvary, and each one of us must experience a personal Calvary again and again. We sing, "Lord, Make Calvary Real to Me," because we know that out of discord comes harmony. There was harmony at Pentecost, and each one of us can experience a personal, progressive Pentecost. We sing, "Lead Me Higher Up the Mountain," because we know the higher the mountain, the greater the view. And the greater the view, the greater our vision.

Sickness can lead to *submission*.

Failure can lead to *success*.

Loss can lead to *serenity*.

Calvary can lead to *salvation*.

Pentecost can lead to *surrender*.

Just ask the Savior and Peter and Stephen.

And the beat goes on!

And when they had set them in the midst, they asked, "By what power or by what name have you done this?"

Then Peter, filled with the Holy Spirit, said to them, "Rulers of the people and elders of Israel: If we this day are judged for a good deed done to a helpless man, by what means he has been made well, let it be known to you all, and to all the people of Israel, that by the name of Jesus Christ of Nazareth, whom you crucified, whom God raised from the dead, by Him this man stands here before you whole. This is the 'stone which was rejected by you builders, which has become the chief cornerstone.'"

—Acts 4:7-11

Two

The Vengeance of Love

Sweet revenge! We have all tasted it vicariously. I have seen Charles Bronson live out my revenge fantasies in *Death Wish I, II, III* and *IV*. I cheered heartily as he mangled successive waves of motorcycle maniacs astride their mighty machines. Somehow, it felt so good to see them annihilated. And why not? We have each been bullied and abused many times in our lives. Most of us crave revenge. Hence, revenge movies are guaranteed winners.

But this is total madness. While Satan condones revenge, Scripture condemns it. Corleone codified it (in *The Godfather*), and Christ was crucified by it. Hell crossed us up with cunning, and Heaven crossed it out with Calvary. In the movie business, Satan, Corleone and Hell are generally money-makers while Scripture, Christ and Heaven are usually busts.

In my more creative moments, I have been contemplating writing a script with a "revenge reversal" theme. The storyline goes something like this:

The Vengeance of Love!

Judge Annas, Sheriff Caiaphas and Alexander, the banker, are in cahoots. Conspiracy and debauchery are their *modus operandi*. They have pillaged the land and plundered the people of Samaria County. Their forte is force, their framework fear. They are unscrupulous and unprincipled, violent and vicious. In response, 12 ragged men from Galilee Junction form a posse of would-be vigilantes. Their leader has been banished, but has vowed to return. They strap on their holsters of hugs, with pistols loaded with kindness. They set out to smother their enemy with kindness, to kill them with kisses and love them to death. But they are mocked and scorned by a jaded public. Only a few are converted to their care; most are not. Over the years their following grows despite overwhelming odds. The suspense builds, the plot thickens and finally their leader returns, bringing justice and judgment. The story climaxes with a thousand-year reign of peace and prosperity.

Sound familiar? It's a movie literally made in Heaven. The message is as timeless as it is matchless. Its plot is unprecedented. Its storyline is unsurpassed. The producer, however, is God, not Darryl Zanuck. It is directed by the Spirit, not Steven Spielberg. It features Christ, not Charlton Heston.

What separates this from all other stories ever written?

What single factor elevates our script into another realm? What is the difference between this story and their story? In Hollywood, the plot usually centers on law and order. In this story, the plot revolves around love and unity. In Hollywood, the vengeance of law is exacted in this life. In this story, the embrace of love is eternal. In Hollywood, the law is supreme. In this story, love is unprecedented. In Hollywood, love is conditional. In this story, love is unconditional. This story is God's story, for its love exacts a unique brand of vengeance:

> *Therefore if your enemy is hungry, feed him; if he is thirsty, give him a drink; for in so doing you will heap coals of fire on his head. Do not be overcome by evil, but overcome evil with good* (Romans 12:20-21).

In another Bible account, Temple leaders unsuccessfully use deception to catch a woman in the act of breaking the law (do not commit adultery) so that He might be caught in the act of disputing that law. The law says there must be an eyewitness to adultery. What better witness than the perpetrator himself? Does the church board call for volunteers? There will be many. Do they draw straws? Many hope for the short one. Do they cast lots? All will be disappointed, save one. It is all a ruse. Thus, the woman is bought so that Christ might be caught:

> *"Now Moses, in the law, commanded us that such should be stoned, but what do You say?" This they said, testing Him* ... (John 8:5-6).

Jesus stoops and scribbles something in the sand. What

is it? Scripture does not say. (That will be one of the many questions I will ask when I get to Heaven.) I believe Jesus wrote *Agape*. "Agape?" they gasp. A tall, skinny Pharisee whispers, "There is no such word. He's stalling for time. We've got him good this time!"

The Hebrew vocabulary did not have a word for unconditional love. A new word has to be invented. Jesus stands and says, "He who is without sin among you, let him throw a stone at her first" (John 8:7).

It works. They walk. God wins. I wonder.

I keep a small pouch in my desk that contains a stone which is inscribed with the words, "the first stone." I had a batch custom-made for a special sermon series. At the conclusion of the series, they were given to each member of the congregation as a reminder of our responsibility to love unconditionally. The pouch teaches that revenge never fulfills. Getting even, in fact, utterly destroys a person.

Love is an effective avenger. Love will win every argument. Love will drive an enemy berserk. Unconditional love!

After Pentecost, Peter responds to those who would punish him to exact the vengeance of man-made law. Peter is a vigilante of love. Peter and John have just healed a man lame from birth. The man asks for alms and receives the balm of Gilead (Jeremiah 8:22). The church leaders feel threatened. They had Peter and John thrown into a dungeon and interrogated:

> *By what power or by what name have you done this?*
> (Acts 4:7).

Peter answers:

> *If we this day are judged for a good deed done to a*
> *helpless man, by what means he has been made well,*
> *let it be known to you all, and to all the people of*
> *Israel, that by the name of Jesus Christ of Nazareth,*
> *whom you crucified, whom God raised from the dead,*
> *by Him this man stands here before you whole*
> (Acts 4:9-10).

They respond in love and are released by the law. Love heals rather than hurts. Love helps rather than hinders. Love hugs rather than hates. Unconditional love cannot be poisoned by the pangs of prejudice. Unconditional love cannot be embittered by the barbs of bile, or altered by the acidity of arrogance.

It's a movie made in Heaven and you too can be a STAR!

Now when they saw the boldness of Peter and John, and perceived that they were uneducated and untrained men, they marveled. And they realized that they had been with Jesus. … And when they had prayed, the place where they were assembled together was shaken; and they were all filled with the Holy Spirit, and they spoke the word of God with boldness.

—Acts 4:13, 31

Three

Gentle Boldness

Boldness has never been one of my more apparent quali-
ties. Had I been a first century disciple, I would have
hung out with Peter. I was a five foot six inch, 99 pound
weakling and now, some 35 years later, I'm a five foot five
inch, 145 pound weakling. For some inexplicable reason, I
have grown and shrunk at the same time.

During the sixties, I was in training to become a Salvation Army officer. One of our most dreaded assignments
was called "buttonholing," confronting potential converts
on the cold-blooded streets of San Francisco. On one of
those frightful expeditions, we emerged from Chinatown
into North Beach. A group of so-called hippies, standing on
the other side of the street, spotted us and yelled, "Come
on over here!"

Inspired by the folk singers Peter, Paul and Mary, we

formed a trio and started singing "Puff the Magic Dragon Lived by the Sea," which became "Jesus Christ of Nazareth Lived by the Sea." After a while, our street corner encounters were amazing. Witnessing was no longer work. It became a worthwhile and meaningful experience. We were soon looking forward to our Monday evening "Hallelujah Hootenannies." We preached the gospel boldly, shouting, "If you don't repent, you're going to hell!" We played and sang loudly, and contrary to what some might have said, our singing was not a sample of what it's going to be like if they go there. We marched into topless nightclubs demanding equal time on their platforms. We proclaimed unabashedly, "We'll show you how to 'take off the old and put on the new.'" We insistently challenged the gurus of a pseudo-intellectual, pot-puffing, pill-popping lifestyle, arguing the case for Christianity from a well-documented, well-rehearsed point of view.

On one occasion, Bud, a fellow cadet, was standing on the fringes listening to our bravado. Bud was about five foot four inches tall, solidly built and with a perpetual grin. He was a good athlete, quick, aggressive and competitive. On the field he was in total control. But in the classroom, he was entirely out of his league.

We were ensconced in debate with a band of bizarre Berkeleyites when Bud stepped forward, hesitatingly, and said gently, "Excuse me. I would just like to say one thing before I leave. I ain't very educated, and I don't understand much of what you're saying. But I know one thing nobody can argue with. Jesus Christ is alive and real. How do I know?

Because He lives within my heart and has changed my life completely."

Bud concluded by saying, "And He can do the same thing for you. God bless you." The silence was deafening. We gulped and turned our eyes downward. A hippie with pierced ears and a purple Nehru jacket broke the silence saying, "Wow! Hey! Cool, man! You can't argue with that." Bud blessed and we blushed.

Bud's boldness was Holy Spirit inspired. Pentecost redefined the meaning of boldness:

> *Now when they saw the boldness of Peter and John, and perceived that they were uneducated and untrained men, they marveled. And they realized that they had been with Jesus* (Acts 4:13).

Boldness in the old sense is Peter recklessly slicing off the soldier's ear. Boldness is Peter walking on water one second and sinking the next. Boldness is Peter irrationally making promises he could not fulfill. Boldness is striking back in anger because of another's sin. Boldness is trusting God in the foxhole and trusting yourself when the battle's won. Boldness is "promising the moon," but believing in gravity.

That was Peter prior to Pentecost. That was Peter without the fire, wind and power. That was Peter before the Holy Spirit took control. God's power brought a new boldness, a gentle boldness that transformed Peter's person, both private and public.

Gentle boldness, on the other hand, is looking the person who just insulted you straight in the eye and saying, "I don't understand, but I love you anyway." Gentle boldness is walking confidently on shaky ground, knowing that the Holy Spirit is beside you.

Gentle boldness is making promises, knowing that they cannot be fulfilled by your own strength. Gentle boldness is trusting God and fighting back when an accident has left you paralyzed from the neck down. Gentle boldness is promising God perfection and letting His Spirit do the perfecting in you. This is every disciple's post-Pentecostal experience, and it begins with a prayer:

> And when they had prayed, the place where they were assembled together was shaken; and they were all filled with the Holy Spirit, and they spoke the word of God with boldness (Acts 4:31).

Gentle boldness is only a prayer away …

Lord,
Shake me down!
Fill me up!
Turn me loose!
Gently … boldly …
Amen.

Even on the streets of San Francisco … if absolutely necessary.

Nor was there anyone among them who lacked; for all who were possessors of lands or houses sold them, and brought the proceeds of the things that were sold, and laid them at the apostles' feet; and they distributed to each as anyone had need.

And Joses, who was also named Barnabas by the apostles (which is translated Son of Encouragement), a Levite of the country of Cyprus, having land, sold it, and brought the money and laid it at the apostles' feet.

—*Acts 4:34-37*

Four

Give and Take

G ive and take is the enduring message of Calvary:

For God so loved the world that He gave His only begotten Son, that whoever believes in [takes] Him should not perish but have everlasting life (John 3:16).

For three years, Jesus preached a "give and take" gospel. Now He gathers His disciples together and unloads a bombshell!

Where I am going you cannot follow Me now, but you shall follow Me afterward (John 13:36b).

They were obviously confused by this statement.

Peter said to Him, "Lord, why can I not follow You now? I will lay down my life for Your sake" (John 13:37).

*Thomas said to Him, "Lord, we do not know where
You are going, and how can we know the way?"*
(John 14:5).

*Philip said to Him, "Lord, show us the Father, and it
is sufficient for us"* (John 14:8).

Is God untrustworthy? Is God taking back His Word?
Why does Christ have to leave?

Jesus said: "And I will pray the Father, and He will give
you another Helper, that He may abide with you forever"
(John 14:16).

There was a great void between Jesus' ascension and
Pentecost. For a moment in time, God squeezed while they
squirmed; lonely and longing, hungering and hoping, griev-
ing and grasping. For a moment in time, they were prophets without power, followers without fellowship, men without a Master.

Why? So they might comprehend the limitation of their
own humanity. So they might fully understand the transi-
tion from a self-centered life to a Spirit-centered life. So
they might grasp the significance of a holy life.

God in the flesh was limited by flesh and blood. He could
only be in one place at a time. He could only perform one
miracle at a time. He could only relate one person at a time.

But God, through the indwelling presence of his Spirit,
is capable of:

Unlimited presence! Unlimited miracles! Unlimited re-
lationships!

This means that all 5,600,000,000—five billion, six hundred million—of us can feel His touch anywhere and every-

where so long as we are aware of His presence in our lives.

Unfortunately, for many there is still a great chasm between Calvary and Pentecost, salvation and holiness, self and others. There are many self-absorbed Christians who have not bridged the gap. There are still some who say, "Give me!" instead of listening to the Spirit who says, "Give Thee!"

The first word that both my boys belted was, "Gimmee!" It began in infancy with, "Whah, ma-ma!" translated, "Gimmee a cuddle, Mom!" In early childhood it turned to, "Gimmee cookies and candy, Mom!" In adolescence it became, "Gimmee the car, Dad!"

In college, the collect call home was always prefaced with a, "Gimmee more cash, Dad!" And before she had her own card, my wife used to say, "Gimmee the credit card, dear!" It took me a while to hear what they were really saying: "Gimmee love, Dad!" I found I wasn't capable of giving them unconditional, non-negotiable love until I took a personal journey to the Upper Room.

The material world advertises, "Take much and give little." Seminars on manipulation, motivation and meditation preach the same mercurial message: "Take it any way you can get it, from anyone who will give it. All you have to do is give them what they think they want, so you can take them for all they have."

The Art of Giving

The widow referenced in Luke 21:1-4 was poor and gave all that she possessed—a grand total of two cents. Her world was not a kind one. Mistreated by many, neglected by society and enslaved by creditors, she was shunned by the government.

Women, whether married or single, were held in low regard in the ancient world, and widows were considered even lower. They had no one to protect or provide for them. They had few mites and virtually no might. And yet this widow gave all that she had.

He was a merchant living in the 20th century. He was rich and gave grudgingly, but he gave away millions. His world is a familiar one. Its standard of living is high and wealth abounds. Tolerated by many, sought after by the masses and worshipped by the church, this man was a creditor who manipulated the government and owned its politicians. As a rich and powerful man, he was held in the highest esteem. He had the Midas touch, and a mighty touch it was.

She gave two cents, and he gave millions. She gave willingly, and he gave grudgingly. He took advantage of others. She gave them the advantage. She gave out of love. He gave out of lust. He took before death and paid after death. She gave before death and was given life after death. He gave to gain power. She gave in response to prayer. On the day of judgment, his life will count for little, hers for much. Their difference was simply this: he took before giving while she gave before taking.

The Joy of Giving

The Pentecostal message says, "You must give before you can take." How much? Everything!

Before Calvary, Jesus said: "And he who does not take

his cross and follow after Me is not worthy of Me" (Matthew 10:38).

After Pentecost, the Holy Spirit inspired Jesus' followers to give "to each as anyone had need" (Acts 4:35b).

Give and take is the herald of holiness. Every human inhabiting this planet, prince or pauper, will experience a need to give and take—whether it be during a great depression, at a death bed confession or upon the receipt of a pink slip. In the final analysis, all will testify to the worthlessness of possessions. Eager to know how much money their late friend had accumulated, one old man whispered to the other, "How much did he leave?" His wiser friend replied, "every last penny." Do not be misled by wealth. Give and take …

For Goodness' Sake!

Yet none of the rest dared join them, but the people esteemed them highly.

—*Acts 5:13*

Five

Lowered to New Heights

Galilee was a ghetto. Nazareth was in Galilee.
Can any good thing come out of Nazareth?
(John 1:46).

The disciples were all Galileans, and as such, were held in low esteem.

They prayed for a Prince.

They sought a Savior.

They cried for a King!

The King of kings came and selected them. He would establish His kingdom. They would become His kingpins.

They waited patiently for their Master to make His move. They studied diligently as their Savior surveyed the scene. They rallied loyally as their Redeemer made Himself ready.

When the time was right, Jesus entered Jerusalem triumphantly!

Their spirits were starting to soar.

Their souls were starting to sing.

The Son was starting to shine.

God made His move at Calvary. He bowed and the finale began. Jesus was lowered to new heights.

"Wait a minute! This isn't according to our script. This isn't what we had in mind! Have we been wasting our time?"

Their spirits sagged.

Their souls sank.

The Son shined.

But the dark clouds would not let the Son shine in. If one could be lower than a Galilean, He was on that day. The disciples had been lowered to new depths.

With Jesus' resurrection, there was a burst of energy. With his sighting, there was a growing optimism. With His ascension, there was mounting vision.

At Pentecost, the spirit soared. They bowed and the fire burned. The disciples were lowered to new heights.

> Then they were all amazed and marveled, saying to one another, "Look, are not all these who speak Galileans?" (Acts 2:7).
>
> … but the people esteemed them highly (Acts 5:13).

––––––––⟨○⟩––––––––

Jonah was being nudged toward Nineveh. "No, no, never, never, uh, uh, uh. Not on your life, Jehovah!" All tied up in knots, he hopped on a boat and took off in the opposite direction at 20 knots. Jonah went down into the lowest part of the ship and fell asleep.

The sea raged!

The skipper was enraged!

Jonah was paged.

"Please engage your God," the captain ordered.

Jonah was tossed overboard, and the tempest turned to calm. A lurking leviathan circled, his hunger unabated. The fish swallowed Jonah whole. Three days and three nights is a long time to spend in a fish's digestive tract.

Needless to say, Jonah had reached the low point of his life. You might even say that he, rather than the whale, had a belly full.

> *And he said, "I cried out to the Lord because of my affliction, and He answered me. Out of the belly of Sheol, I cried and You heard my voice"* (Jonah 2:2).

He bowed and the fish brought forth. Jonah was lowered to new heights.

> *You have brought up my life from the pit, O Lord, my God* (Jonah 2:6).

———◄○►———

Like the disciples, I was seeking recognition from the man rather than the Master. Achievement, appointment and applause were Joe's masters. Like Jonah, Joe was running for selfish reasons rather than for spiritual results. Fear, faithlessness and foolishness were my masters.

Like the disciples and countless Jonahs down through the centuries, God had to get my attention. Like Jesus, the disciples and Jonah, he took me deep down into the bowels of Sheol, into the belly of Beelzebub himself. I tasted the acrid elixir of death.

I wasn't a lost sinner. I was a lousy saint. I had put the Savior on the shelf as a convenient concordance to be used on those rare occasions when my own efforts seemed to fail. My heart was right, but my head was wrong.

I went for my annual physical. The battery of tests signaled the need for a biopsy. From the moment the doctor said malignancy, my world turned upside down. There were tests and waiting. More tests and more waiting. Finally came the surgery and more waiting. During this time I sank to the lowest low I had ever experienced.

I bowed and the Father blessed. Joe was lowered to new heights.

The final laboratory results came in. The doctor called and said, "I am so excited and happy to give you this good news. You passed the test, and the cure is complete. It looks like you're going to live another 30 or 40 years." My wife said, "Better get it in writing."

Another kind of test will be even more significant: the one that determines whether you live or die in eternity. I want to hear the Savior say, "I am so excited and happy to give you this good news. All of the results are in and you passed the test. You are going to live forever, as your name is written in the Book of Life."

Well done good and faithful servant (Matthew 25:23).

P.S. I've got it in writing!

So that they brought the sick out into the streets and laid them on beds and couches, that at least the shadow of Peter passing by might fall on some of them.

—Acts 5:15

Six

Brilliant Shadows

There was a gigantic oak tree growing in front of our house. Its size, no doubt, exaggerated by memory. Somehow, objects always get magnified by the wide, curious eyes of an 8-year-old. My front yard seemed the size of a baseball field, especially when it had to be mowed and trimmed. In reality, it was probably no larger than home plate. Nevertheless, that yard and tree hold happy memories for me. I spent countless hours hidden in the shadow of that tree, exploring its branches.

It was a "hoping place" where I could dream wild things and make grand wishes. In that tree I became a gladiator savoring his latest victory. In that tree I became an explorer, searching beyond the sunset. In that tree I was a little boy wishing upon a star.

It was my "hiding place" where I thought my deepest

thoughts and held my most sequestered secrets. I thought about heaven. "Would the lion really lie down with the lamb? Would my dog be there? Would I be there?" I thought about hell. "How hot is it? Does the devil really have horns? I don't want to go there!" I thought about me. "Why did I lie to my mother? Is there really a devil on one shoulder and an angel on the other whispering in each ear? Why is the devil louder?"

It was my "healing place" where I nursed hurts and shed tears. "Why do Mommy and Daddy argue so much? Why does Mommy cry all of the time? Why doesn't Daddy play with me? What's the matter with me, Lord?"

One day, some strange men came and chopped the tree down. My sanctuary was gone. Its mosaic shadows no longer fell. There was no shade.

Shadows are a curious thing. They provide a place of refuge from the scorching heat. They brighten the soul and ignite the spirit. They prepare us for the sun:

> They brought the sick out into the streets and laid them on beds and couches, that at least the shadow of Peter passing by might fall on some of them. Also, a multitude gathered from the surrounding cities to Jerusalem, bringing sick people and those who were tormented by unclean spirits, and they were all healed (Acts 5:15-16).

The man had lived in darkness from birth (Mark 8:22-26). He could not comprehend the brilliance of the sun. Another's sound was his sonar. Another's light was his beam. Another's arm was his candle. They guided the blind man to

Jesus. He was totally dependent upon others. He was, in a word, "other-wise."

I was at The Salvation Army's Central Corps in Mexico City at a New Year's Eve party when they blindfolded me. The crowd encouraged me to hit the piñata hard enough to release all of its "goodies" inside. No problem! A piece of cake, or at least a piece of the piñata, I thought. I lifted the stick confidently. Several pairs of hands guided me in circles until I was totally disoriented. When they released me, I started swinging wildly. Nothing! The crowd laughed and started to chant, "Arriba! Arriba!" I reached higher and swung the stick. Laughter! "Arriba! Arriba!" I staggered and swung. I swaggered and swung. I swatted and swung. It was always the same. Nothing! Laughter! "Arriba! Arriba!" I was totally dependent upon the sound and touch of others. In other words, I was "other-wise."

Jesus led the blind man out of town in another direction. With a gentle touch, He removed the blindfold and said, "Do you see anything?" He looked out and said, "I see men like trees walking." There was now a bright shadow.

I felt a touch, and the blindfold was removed. My sight was blurred. My balance was shaky. Amazingly, my back was to the piñata! I had been swinging at trees lining the courtyard wall.

In the distance, the blind man saw a ray of hope, a sheen of light. There was a glimmer, a promise. A second touch restored his vision fully. Suddenly night turned into day. He saw everyone and everything clearly for the first time in his life.

I watched others take their turn at the piñata. Just prior to midnight, they decided to give me, their guest, a second chance. This time their touch pointed me in the right direction. "Arriba! Arriba!" I stretched. I swung. I smashed the piñata, spraying its contents in every direction. After removing the blindfold, I saw clearly that everyone savored my success. They even saved a bit of the bounty for me.

Being blindfolded prepared me for eventual success. The shadow prepared the blind man for the sun and the Son.

Isaiah prophetically announced the Messiah's mission: "In the shadow of His hand He has hidden me."

That promise was fulfilled in the shadow of the cross, His first touch: "And made Me a polished shaft" (Isaiah 49:2).

That promise was fulfilled in the fire of Pentecost, His second touch: "Then there appeared to them divided tongues as a fire, and one sat upon each of them. And they were all filled with the Holy Spirit" (Acts 2:3-4).

The shadow of Peter represented the brilliance of the fire of the Holy Spirit. Since that day, there have been many bright shadows shedding light upon a darkened world.

What is the state of your spiritual shadow? I like to think of mine as a sanctified shadow—always preparing someone for the Son.

Oh, lest you were saddened by the removal of my special tree, I soon found an even better one. Soon after my tree was felled, some friends invited me to Sunday school at The Salvation Army, and I climbed into the ...

Tree of Life!

And when they had brought them, they set them before the council. And the high priest asked them, saying, "Did we not strictly command you not to teach in this name? And look, you have filled Jerusalem with your doctrine, and intend to bring this Man's blood on us!"

But Peter and the other apostles answered and said: "We ought to obey God rather than men. The God of our fathers raised up Jesus whom you murdered by hanging on a tree. Him God has exalted to His right hand to be Prince and Savior, to give repentance to Israel and forgiveness of sins. And we are His witnesses to these things, and so also is the Holy Spirit whom God has given those who obey Him."

When they heard this, they were furious and plotted to kill them. Then one in the council stood up, a Pharisee named Gamaliel, a teacher of the law held in respect by all the people, and commanded them to put the apostles outside for a little while. And he said to them: "Men of Israel, take heed to yourselves what you intend to do regarding these men. For some time ago Theudas rose up, claiming to be somebody. A number of men, about four hundred, joined him. He was slain, and all who obeyed him were scattered and came to nothing. After this man, Judas of Galilee rose up in the days of the census, and drew away many people after him. He also perished, and all who obeyed him were dispersed. And now I say to you, keep away from these men and let them alone; for if this plan or this work is of men, it will come to nothing; but if it is of God, you cannot overthrow it—lest you even be found to fight against God."

—Acts 5:27-39

Seven

Defiant Obedience

Peter and the other apostles are about to make a power play. They are not posturing for position. Nor are they pressing for prestige or plotting for power. In fact, they are programming themselves for prison. This particular power play has been orchestrated by God and has a happy ending.

The apostles are seated before the Hebrew Council when the following question is asked: "Did we not strictly command you not to teach in this name?"

They answered: "We ought to obey God rather than men."

Now if that isn't enough to get them into trouble, their next statement is a prison clincher.

They continue: "The God of our Fathers raised up Jesus whom you murdered by hanging on a tree."

They conclude the response by revealing the source of

their power, namely: "The Holy Spirit, whom God has given
to those who obey Him."

In other words, without obedience to God there is no
power. The disciples put their power up against that of the
high priests in a courtroom drama. The council is furious
and calls for the death penalty. Gamaliel, a respected teacher
of the law, is the public defender. He begins by presenting a
pair of precedents. The first is "Theudas versus the people."

Gamaliel argues: "Theudas rose up claiming to be somebody. A number of men, about four hundred, joined him.
He was slain, and all who obeyed him were scattered and
came to nothing."

The second is Judas of Galilee, who amassed a great
following.

Gamaliel continues: "He also perished, and all who
obeyed him were disbursed."

His closing argument is delivered with brilliance and
inspiration:

> And now I say to you, keep away from these men and
> let them alone; for if this plan or this work is of men,
> it will come to nothing; but if it is of God, you cannot
> overthrow it—lest you even be found to fight against
> God (Acts 5:28-39).

What is Gamaliel's strategy? He "entangles them in their
talk." What does Gamaliel say? He says, in so many words,
"We ought to obey God rather than men." The prosecution
is beaten logically and worthily. The disciples are beaten
physically, counting it worthy.

There is another Teacher of the law who finds Himself

in a similar position, except that He was both defendant and defender. The prosecution plots to "entangle Him in His talk." The prosecution tarries with flattery and finesse. The prosecution prods with a question of entrapment: "What do You think? Is it lawful to pay taxes to Caesar, or not?"

They hope that what begins with a test will end with a trial. They pray that this interrogation will precede an internment. They expect their inquiry to precipitate an inquest.

The Defendant responds: "Why do you test Me, you hypocrites? Show Me the tax money … Whose image and inscription is this?"

The prosecution counters confidently: "Caesar's."

His closing argument goes beyond brilliance, "Render therefore to Caesar the things that are Caesar's, and to God the things that are God's" (Matthew 22:17-21).

Jesus is marvelous, and the Pharisees are impressed. Please note that He does not say, "Give unto Caesar the things that are God's." That would be in direct opposition to the law of God. Defiant obedience comes when man's law is in conflict with God's law and we side with the latter.

Defiant obedience is not a demonstration of force. Defiant obedience is not a demonstration against the law of man. Defiant obedience is a demonstration for peace. Defiant obedience is a demonstration for the law of God.

It must be understood clearly that, in both instances, the prosecution represents the religious hierarchy. That same danger exists today. We must be careful not to twist the Word of God. We must be careful not to obey man's law when it is in contradiction to God's law. We must be careful not to give unto Caesar that which belongs to God.

We dare not compromise the law of God with the traditions of men. We dare not rationalize religion in order to defy the I.R.S. We dare not subvert religion to deify the golden calf. We dare not rationalize religion to indemnify ourselves against persecution and death.

Religion is ritual that can be managed by humans or ritual that can be managed for the Master. Religion is law ordered by a host of lords or law ordained by the Lord of Hosts. Religion is the law authored by God and finished by man, or the law authored by Christ and finished by Him through faith.

The choice, inevitably, is mine:

How I worship.

How I witness.

How I walk.

How we choose to live our lives is the burning question that unites all individuals, through all time and in all places.

Is my lifestyle a litany of lamentation? Do I worship with hymns of hypocrisy?

"Imagine letting those homeless people worship with us. What a disgrace! I think the pastor's off-base."

Then Jesus, moved with compassion, stretched out His hand and touched him (Mark 1:41).

"John has his nerve to suggest that we change the time for Sunday evening service. He thinks we can attract new people. Huh! We are happy just the way we are, thank you!

And besides, if it was good enough for our grandparents, it's good enough for the four of us!"

> *He said to them, "All too well you reject the commandment of God, that you may keep your tradition"* (Mark 7:9).

"I have been asked to set up the Saturday visitation team. Can you believe that? Sacrifice my Saturdays? I already give up my Sundays for church."

> *If anyone desires to come after me, let him deny himself and take up his cross, and follow Me* (Matthew 16:24).

Or is my lifestyle a litany of love? Do I worship with hymns of holiness?

The lifestyle of Jesus is one of obedience to God. Obedience provides a touchstone in times of turmoil. Obedience reduces risk because it's right. Obedience is denial of self and a desire for the cross.

Lass was a last-minute Christmas present for my wife. I deposited the money for the playful pup on Christmas Eve, and was on my way to drop her off at a friend's house when she left a deposit on the front seat of my car. And the deposits didn't end there, either.

I have a very traditional approach to deposit training: Rub! Smack! Rub! But Doris is a little more compassionate and progressive. She enrolled the dog in an obedience training class. My wife was taught to "Touch! Praise! Touch!" She was taught that patience, commitment and discipline are essential elements to successful obedience training. To my amazement, the pup responded slowly but surely to the touch of the master's hand. She began to sit, stay, heel and deposit with proper canine deportment.

Our neighborhood organization has an annual dog show, and every entry wins a prize. We thought it would be cute to have our 7-year-old son put Lass through her paces. He took the leash and gave the command, "Heel!" Lass pulled and Robby pulled. The dog won the tug of war, dragging Robby across the field on his heels. Doris took command, and with her masterful touch, this hyperkinetic canine became a thoroughly pacified pet. To our surprise, Lass won two ribbons: "Most Obedient Dog" and "Strongest Dog."

We have a choice. We can pull or perform. The first requires our own strength. The second requires the Master's touch. Obedience to the love of God is always a …

Touching Experience!

And they [the Council] agreed with him [Gamaliel], and when they had called for the apostles and beaten them, they commanded that they should not speak in the name of Jesus, and let them go. So they departed from the presence of the council, rejoicing that they were counted worthy to suffer shame for His name.

—*Acts 5:40-41*

Eight

Shameful Worthiness

The Council was beaten worthily, and the apostles were beaten, counting it worthy.

So they departed from the presence of the Council, rejoicing that they were counted worthy to suffer shame (Acts 5:41).

Now there's a switch. True greatness is counting it worthy to suffer shame? True greatness is counting it worthy to be beaten badly? True greatness is counting it worthy to be humiliated harshly?

Why didn't somebody tell me this when I had my first playground confrontation with the school bully? Why didn't somebody tell me this when I single-handedly humiliated myself and the entire team by muffing a ground ball that cost the championship? Why didn't somebody tell me this during all of the tiresome "shame on yous" suffered during my troubled childhood and adolescence?

Had I known, I would have treated each situation dif-
ferently. I would have thanked the bully publicly, saying,
"By giving me this black eye, bruised lip and bloody nose,
you have made me feel wonderful and worthy." I would have
leaped and "high fived" all of my teammates, shouting "It's
not often that you get the opportunity to blow a championship game. I'm experiencing an incredible high right now!"
When caught lying to my mother, I would have lifted my
head in shame, crying, "Thank you, Mother, for catching
me in this deceitful act. Its very shame gives me an over-
powering sense of humiliation."

But wait a minute! Paul doesn't end his verse there.
Three critical words complete his text—"for His name."

The greatest victory ever won was accomplished in defeat, not for the sake of defeat, but for goodness' sake. The
greatest moment in history was spent in shame, not for the
sake of shame, but for goodness' sake. The greatest hope
we have was fashioned in humiliation, not for the sake of
humiliation, but for goodness' sake.

Jesus died on the cross for our sake. His apparent and
temporary defeat was only a momentary pause in time, so
long as we allow the Spirit of God to go on perfecting His
plan in us.

> Let us fix our eyes on Jesus, the Author and Perfecter
> of our faith, who for the joy set before Him endured
> the cross, scorning its shame, and sat down at the
> right hand of the throne of God (Hebrews 12:2, NIV).

To the Christian, the cross is a symbol of hope and direction. "And anyone who does not take his cross and follow Me is not worthy of Me" (Matthew 10:38, NIV). To the Romans, the cross was a symbol of shame and destruction. To the righteous, the cross is a symbol of surrender and victory, where you shed your shame and find life everlasting.

The cross was expected.

The cross was endured.

The cross was transformed by the Son of God.

The words "mock," "scourge" and "crucify" are a part of His prophetic vocabulary. Common criminals were hung in disgrace. Jesus was hung because of God's grace. Victims were crucified in their shame. Jesus was crucified in God's name. The guilty died because of their sins. The guiltless one died because of our sin.

The thief on one side was insulted by Christ's presence and said, "I beg your pardon!" The thief on the other side accepted His divinity and pleaded, "I beg your pardon" (Luke 24:39-43). In one moment, Jesus was nailed to the cross in seeming shame. In the next, He had surmounted the cross in permanent victory.

Many of you have experienced the agony of victory; some have not.

Many of you can identify with a parent who has agonized over a child. The child who was given every advantage took total advantage of everyone else. His habits were compulsive; her actions were impulsive; his lifestyle was repulsive. She was pigheaded, and he was big-headed. She was found wanting. He was found wasting (Luke 15:11-17).

Some of you can identify with those prodigal children.

You also might want to wail, "Father, I am no longer worthy to be called Your child" (my paraphrase).

No lectures. No penalties. No conditions. Just love and acceptance:

> *"For this my son was dead and is alive again, he was lost and is found." And they began to be merry* (Luke 15:24).

This spiritual drama has the potential to be played out in your life, if it hasn't already. The cross is a symbol of surrender, the only place where you can shed yourself and count it worthy to suffer shame—for His name.

The world would consider it a shame, a waste, a sham! But God knows it is a sign of true greatness and real power. To suffer along the way is to triumph in the end. Are you suffering a little discomfort for Christ's sake? If not ...

Shame on You!

Part 2

—◁◦▷—

Great Grace

And great grace was upon them all (Acts 4:33b).

Spontaneous Spiritual Compassion

The Apostle Paul captured the essence of spontaneous spiritual compassion when he wrote:

> *That in the ages to come He might show the exceeding riches of His grace in His kindness toward us in Christ Jesus. For by grace you have been saved through faith, and that not of yourselves; it is the gift of God* (Ephesians 2:7-8).

There is nothing more spontaneous than the grace of God. When our penitence is deliberate, His response is immediate and automatic. In these circumstances grace is a reciprocal act of love. Give love and it will be given in return. The more you give, the more you will get. Grace is the foundation for forgiveness. Grace is the "forget" in forgiveness. Grace is the "favor" in forgiveness. Grace is the "gift" in gospel. It is given freely and unselfishly.

One Christmas, I gave my wife a kitten. That was a mistake because, unfortunately, the kitten soon became a cat. This particular feline was ill-conceived, ill-tempered and ill-litter-ate. And I was ill at ease around it.

On the other hand, my wife loved that cat. She played with it and pampered it. She cuddled it, stroked it, nuzzled it. And the cat did nothing for her in return. Still she fed it, picked up after it, cleaned its litter box, and still that ungrateful cat gave absolutely nothing back. All it did was tear up the paper (before I had a chance to read it), rip up the curtains, and sit in my special chair whenever it pleased. But my wife loved it anyway.

This may not be the perfect example of God's grace, but my wife loved that cat the way God loves us—in spite of ourselves, in spite of our behavior, in spite of our selfishness.

Now, if I had fed, cleaned, played with, pampered, cuddled, stroked and nuzzled that cat, feeling the way I do about cats generally, that would be a purr-fect example of ...

Great Grace!

Now in those days, when the number of the disciples was multiplying, there arose a complaint against the Hebrews by the Hellenists, because their widows were neglected in the daily distribution. Then the twelve summoned the multitude of the disciples and said, "It is not desirable that we should leave the word of God and serve tables. Therefore, brethren, seek out from among you seven men of good reputation, full of the Holy Spirit and wisdom, whom we may appoint over this business; but we will give ourselves continually to prayer and the ministry of the word."

And the saying pleased the whole multitude. And they chose Stephen, a man full of faith and the Holy Spirit, and Philip, Prochorus, Nicanor, Timon, Parmenas, and Nicolas, a proselyte from Antioch, whom they set before the apostles; and when they had prayed, they laid hands on them.

Then the word of God spread, and the number of the disciples multiplied greatly in Jerusalem, and a great many of the priests were obedient to the faith.

—Acts 6:1-6

Nine

First to be Last

The church flourished. The congregation complained. The cabinet caucused.

A bold new business plan was written. A whole new management level was created. A bright new leadership team was mandated. An employment notice was issued:

WANTED: Seven sanctified souls for newly-created service manager positions. Must be men of good reputation, full of the Holy Spirit and full of wisdom.

The leadership team was selected: Stephen, Philip, Prochorus, Nicanor, Timon, Paramenas and Nicolas.

They organized.

They prioritized.

They advertised (Acts 6:1-6):

WANTED: Service Representatives. A position guaranteed for every qualified applicant. Unlimited opportunity. No pay. Long hours. Hard work.

QUALIFICATIONS:

   Must possess a thick skin and soft heart.
   Must always be the first to be last.
   Must be capable of giving out without giving in.
   Must be willing to give all that you have.
   Must be faithful, fervent and friendly.
   Must be on call 24 hours a day.
   Humility helpful.
   Grace necessary.
   Knee pads essential.
   Salvation will ensure job security.

BENEFITS: An insurance and retirement plan that is out of this world. Satisfaction guaranteed. Apply in person to the Holy Spirit.

   And great grace was upon them all (Acts 4:33b).

Certainly charity began prior to these chosen men. But on that day, the role of servanthood took on a whole new dimension. On that day, service to God and man became a revolutionary force for compassionate change in our society. Martin Luther comprehended its power. John Wesley captured its essence. William Booth caught its vision. Charity is love in action. God is love. Charity cannot exist apart from God.

I was born in Mercy Hospital, San Diego, California, and my wife was born in Grace Hospital, Winnepeg, Manitoba, Canada. Someone has said, "Justice is getting what you deserve. Mercy is not getting what you deserve.

And grace is getting what you don't deserve." If my logic is correct, Doris' parents got what they didn't deserve, and my parents didn't get what they deserved. My two sons were born in Good Samaritan Hospital, and during their adolescent years, I came to understand fully the meaning of what it takes to be a good Samaritan.

And speaking of two sons, the mother of James and John came to Jesus with an interesting request. She had the audacity to kneel down before Jesus and, in front of all the other disciples, ask, "Grant that these two sons of mine may sit, one on Your right hand and the other on the left, in Your Kingdom" (Matthew 20:21).

She was suffering from a very serious affliction—son blindness.

Moms are like that you know!

Most mothers suffer from blind spots, and the mother of my two sons is no exception.

When I would accuse them of being lazy, she argued that a growth spurt was sapping their strength. When I suggested they clean their plate, she insisted that this would happen naturally when they entered a growth spurt. When I choked on the credit card bill, she calmly stated that the clothing was necessary because of a growth spurt. As they grew, I groaned. They sprouted. I pouted, "When will this ever end? My sons are now 22 and 24 years old!"

The other day, my wife asked firmly, "Joe, would you take out the trash, please?" I answered meekly, "But I am going through a growth spurt, you know!" "Go on," she said incredulously, "You don't have growth spurts at your age!"

And I said, "Not according to Mother."

Moms are like that, you know!

I wouldn't be surprised if my wife has secretly prayed, "Grant that these two sons of mine may sit, one on Your right hand and the other on the left, in Your Kingdom."

"You don't know what you are asking, Mom," Jesus responds. "You had better think this over," He implies. Then comes the clincher: "Are you able to drink the cup that I am about to drink, and be baptized with the baptism I am baptized with?"

The disciples, each clamoring for the seat of honor, answered unanimously and naively, "We are able!" (Matthew 20:22).

Let me paraphrase how I think Jesus handled this potentially explosive situation.

"Step over here boys. Listen, the mother of James and John means well. She wants the best for her children."

Moms are like that, you know!

"But let Me tell you something about cup drinking and fire baptism," He continued. "Let Me explain what it means to get your feet wet. Let Me give you a lecture on price paying and power playing. When I talk about greatness, I use words like grace, mercy, love and servant. You will never hear Me use words like aspiration, success, ambition and superior. That's the world's view. Greatness is not about might.

"Come closer. Listen clearly to the lesson of your life:"

Whoever desires to become great among you, let him
be your servant. And whoever desires to be first

among you, let him be your slave—just as the Son of
Man did not come to be served, but to serve, and to
give His life a ransom for many (Matthew 20:26-28).

Jesus understood what it meant to be great. Follow His advice, and I will guarantee you a growth spurt that will last forever—a growth spurt to greatness.

Jesus is like that, you know!

And Stephen, full of faith and power, did great wonders and signs among the people.

—Acts 6:8

Ten

Common Wonders

Stephen was a wonder to behold. He was appointed, anointed, and Stephen, "full of faith and power, did great wonders and signs among the people" (Acts 6:8). Signs and wonders were commonplace in the life of Stephen.

There is a subtle synchronization present between "faith" and "grace" as the two blend naturally together:

> *For by grace are ye saved through faith; and that not of yourselves: it is the gift of God* (Ephesians 2:8, KJV).

Stephen performed signs and wonders because he received grace through faith. And the connection is always made through prayer. Do you pray and wonder? Or do you pray expecting a wonder?

I wonder.

Faith is expecting the unexpected. How much faith is needed? The disciples suspected that Christ expected a lot more faith than they had. "Lord, increase our faith," they said. He said, in so many words, "You already have enough faith to replant a mulberry tree without touching it" (Luke 17:5-6). "Lord, why can't we cast the demons out," they said. He said, "Because you are not exercising what little faith you have. You already have enough faith to move a mountain" (Matthew 17:19-21).

The secret is found in the exercise, and this kind of faith must be exercised through prayer. Are you getting the right kind of exercise?

I wonder.

As a youth I could easily identify with Old Mother Hubbard. Those were "bare cupboard" days, but I was bound and determined to attend Bible college. I begged and borrowed the first semester's tuition, and my freshman year began. Every morning, I found myself sitting in chapel, listening to others tell the same story with one or two variables. The testimonies went something like this: "I was going to drop out of school because of financial difficulty. I prayed one final, desperate prayer asking the Lord to send me (the amount varied) by (the date varied). Several days later, I went to my mailbox and there was an anonymous letter with a money order in the exact amount I had prayed for!" Coincidence or confirmation? I wonder.

"That beats working," I mumbled to myself. "Might as well give it a try. Got nothing to lose," I reasoned. So I prayed, "Lord, send me $100 by November 15th." I went to the mailbox on the appointed day. Nothing! I tried for $50. Nothing! $25. Nothing! I tried God's patience. He tried my faith.

I prayed, "Lord, what am I doing wrong?" I opened my Bible to page 1093. There it was.

Thomas was troubled: "Lord, we do not know where You are going, and how can we know the way?"

Philip needed proof: "Lord, show us the Father, and it is sufficient for us."

Judas wanted justification: "Lord, how is it that You will manifest Yourself to us, and not to the world?" (John 14:5, 8, 22).

Jesus said, "Most assuredly, I say to you, he who believes in me, the works that I do he will do also; and greater works than these he will do, because I go to My Father" (John 14:12).

Greater works I will do? What? When? How? Read on.

Believe in Me …

Ask anything …

In My name …

Keep My commandments … (John 14:11-15).

In these verses, the Lord revealed His "greater works" (great wonders) formula to me.

Keep My commandments

Spring revival meetings had just concluded. The Holy Spirit did a work in me, and I was broke and broken but happy. I believed in Him. It was spring break, and I had loaded my 1939 Chevrolet sedan with every possession I owned.

The tires were tired. The brakes were bleeding. The paint was peeling.

But it was mine—free and clear! It was dark when I

started the long journey home. About midway, in the middle of nowhere, "Jezebel" (she was always betraying me) started to spit and sputter. I looked, and the needle was on empty. What happened to the twenty-five cents' worth I had put in last week? There were no gas stations. There was no money to buy gas. There were no telephone booths. There was nobody to call. "What am I going to do?" I cried out. He said, "Ask anything."

Out of desperation, I prayed, "Lord, just get me to within one block of my home, please!" A ridiculous request you say? It was simple, spontaneous, sincere and uttered in His Name.

When I said, "Lord," it was not in vain. When I said, "Lord," it was with clear recognition of the One to whom I was speaking. When I said, "Lord," we were of one accord and I believed in Him.

I didn't have time to doubt. There was no inclination to question the legitimacy of my request. It didn't occur to me that I should just throw my hands up in vain and coast to the side of the road. I simply prayed and envisioned the car coasting to a stop on that street corner one block from my house. Then I pressed the pedal to the metal. On that day, I learned that there are five components to faith: surrender, belief, vision, action and persistence. Christ illustrates this fifth part in His Parable of the Persistent Friend who didn't relent until his plea was heard and acted upon (Luke 11:5-10).

I pushed, and the car coughed.

I pressed, and the engine sputtered.

I persisted, and the power ignited.

The engine purred peacefully until it stopped—where? You guessed it. Right on the very street corner I had envisioned during my prayer. Coincidence or confirmation? I wonder!

I don't wonder anymore in a questioning way. I wonder with an exclamation point! And if you're still wondering why, read on!

And Stephen, full of faith and power, did great wonders and signs among the people.

—*Acts 6:8*

Eleven

More Wonders

The "greater works" formula has continued over the years. Its effectiveness and quantity depends upon the state of my spiritual condition and concentration. The following is one example out of many.

I was coerced into producing and directing, on a small budget, a "spectacular" show in Macomb, Illinois, although I was living in California. "Small" and "spectacular" are obviously not synonymous. I reminded the backers that "substantial" was still considered a legitimate word in *Webster's New Collegiate Dictionary*. I quickly learned that "ledgers" and "dictionaries" were not synonymous either. I was informed that the word no is clearly understood in every language. And I was soon to learn that Macomb is the absolute antonym for Hollywood in terms of American cities. The only thing they have in common is that in both places, the stars come out at night. In other words, I was being asked to do the impossible.

I flew to Illinois, and we drove through two hundred miles of nothing but cornfields before reaching the show venue and sight of our first production meeting. I had already determined that a llama was needed for the South American scene, and "cornfield" and "llama" are not synonymous either. I was strongly advised to rewrite the script. "You'll never find a llama in the middle of Illinois," my production team echoed unanimously.

I prayed and a llama brayed as we passed a farm on the outskirts of Macomb. "Would it be possible to rent a llama for our show?" I begged.

"We can give you papa llamas, mama llamas, baby llamas, a whole train of llamas," the farm owners said excitedly.

"How much?" I muttered warily.

"Nothing. You can have them for free!" they exclaimed.

"Wonderful!" I cried.

The script also called for a covered wagon, horses and Indians. The budget called for help. "You'll never find horses, riders, covered wagons and Indians in the middle of Illinois. And if by chance you did, the cost would be prohibitive," my production team echoed unanimously.

The llama people knew a man who had just finished building a covered wagon, and they could find horses and plenty of riders ... for free. "We would be honored if you would let us ride in your show," they said. "Wonderful!" I cried.

You're not going to believe this, but the script also called for elephants and camels. And, yes, the budget still called for help. "Show me," my production team said skeptically. The llama ranchers said they knew a man just across the border in Missouri (the "Show Me" state) who would bring elephants and camels "just for the cost of transportation." "Wonderful!" I cried.

A space creature was the star of our show, and a customized costume was needed. Some preliminary investigation indicated that this would be a very expensive proposition indeed.

Every theatre and costume-maker we contacted referred us to the same source, Don Post Studios in Hollywood. I called. He said come. "The costume will cost about $8,000 to create," he guessed. He debated. I waited. He was weighing. I was praying. After what seemed an eternity, he said, "I'll make you a deal. My company is going through a financial crisis right now. I must make an important decision next week that will mean the difference between bankruptcy and solvency. You pray for me, and I will make the costume." "Wonderful!" I said. "Let's pause for prayer right now." I prayed and the bills were paid as the costume was made. "We thought it might turn out that way," my production team said sheepishly.

The finale called for fireworks. They were set for our display. The fire marshall was set in his way, "No, no, no! The fireworks must be moved behind the stadium!" he stated adamantly.

I prayed and the marshall was swayed. That evening the fireworks were arrayed and His Spirit was displayed, to the edification and enjoyment of ALL.

"There was absolutely no question about it," my production team said. "Let's do another show with people who fly, pythons, indoor fireworks, lasers and the Pope!" And we did!

Wonders come in every shape and size. Some are simple. Some are spectacular. Some are little. Some are large. But they all have one thing in common. They are commonplace in the life of any Christian who puts into practice the "greater works" formula.

"I wonder?" should never be a question. "I wonder!" should always be an exclamation. You should never say, "Show me," like Thomas did before Pentecost. You should always pray, "Show me!" like Stephen did after Pentecost. You will quickly find that "grace" and "greatness" are synonymous.

Prayer:

> Lord,
> I obey.
>   I ask …
> in your Name.
> I believe.
> Show me!
> Amen.

Praise:

> I wonder!

Then there arose some from what is called the Synagogue of the Freedmen (Cyrenians, Alexandrians, and those from Cilicia and Asia), disputing with Stephen. And they were not able to resist the wisdom and the Spirit by which he spoke. Then they secretly induced men to say, "We have heard him speak blasphemous words against Moses and God." And they stirred up the people, the elders, and the scribes; and they came upon him, seized him, and brought him to the council. They also set up false witnesses who said, "This man does not cease to speak blasphemous words against this holy place and the law; for we have heard him say that this Jesus of Nazareth will destroy this place and change the customs which Moses delivered to us."

—Acts 6:9-14

Twelve

Love and Hate

Stephen spoke. The council swore. Stephen preached. The council plotted. Stephen seized the opportunity. The council seized Stephen. Stephen persisted. The council perjured. The council stirred. Stephen smiled. "And all who sat in the council, looking steadfastly at him, saw his face as the face of an angel" (Acts 6:15).

The high priest begins the interrogation saying, "Are these things so?" Instead of pleading the fifth amendment, Stephen takes the next 50 verses to remind them from whence they came. He preaches expositorily from their scriptures to set the record straight. Without mincing words, he methodically addresses the sins of "our fathers." Suddenly, without warning or compromise, he dramatically drives the message home in three short verses, saying:

You stiff-necked [people] and uncircumcised in heart

and ears! You always resist the Holy Spirit; as your fathers did, so do you. Which of the prophets did your fathers not persecute? And they killed those who foretold the coming of the Just One, of whom you now have become the betrayers and murderers, who have received the law by the direction of angels and have not kept it (Acts 7:51-53).

How did the Council react to these honest accusations? How would you react? Be honest. With rage? Fury? Hate?

And Stephen, being full of the Holy Spirit, surprised them again by gazing heavenward and saying, "Look! I see the heavens opened and the Son of Man standing at the right hand of God!" (Acts 7:56).

That was the proverbial straw that broke the camel's back, salt rubbed into an open wound, a modern day "in your face." That was not Stephen's intent, but it was their interpretation. Impulsively and with one accord, they cried out loud, covered their ears and cast him outside where they began to stone him.

Then Stephen did something amazing. The one who had been uncompromising, the one who had spoken the truth firmly, the one who "told it like it is" surprised them again by crying out with a loud voice, saying, "Lord, do not charge them with this sin" (Acts 7:60).

He had learned his lesson well. He was imitating the Master. This was the consummate example of love in action—unconditional and universal. Jesus taught him to hate the sin and love the sinner. Hating the sin is a sign of strength. Loving the sinner is an act of gentleness and greatness.

How did he do that, you say? How does one distinguish between the sin and the sinner?

Sometimes, as parents, we face the same dilemma. Take the area of cleanliness. My wife was brought up quite properly and taught that "cleanliness is next to godliness." On the other hand, I was raised with the philosophy that "a little dirt is good for the soul."

As parents of two active boys, we were often guilty of not being able to separate the soot from the son. Have you ever said to your child, "Now you can go out and play, but don't get dirty, because we are going to church (or wherever) tonight"? Sure! That's like telling a bird not to fly, a fish not to swim, a pig not to wallow.

Now you're supposed to hate the soot and love your son. You're supposed to separate your feelings toward the soot from your feelings toward your son. That's easy to do the first fifteen times, and then the line begins to blur.

When my son and his friends would climb into the van after a baseball game, and that pungent, pervasive sweat odor filled my wife's nostrils until it permeated the very essence of her soul, she couldn't wait to get the boy into the shower and herself into the tub. This happened so many times that she christened him the "Prince of Tide." In fact, the tide goes out very quickly (much more quickly than the dirt), threatening to take one's sanity with it. She would exclaim, "I can't take it anymore." I'd begin to worry, and the dog would hide. She stated loudly, "I hate dirt." I breathed a sigh of relief, and the dog re-appeared. My son began to cry because he thought that she hated him. She immediately took that smelly little body into her arms and said, "No, honey, I love you very much." She paused, took a deep breath, and said between gritted teeth, "It's the dirt I detest!"

It is a very thin and delicate line that separates the soot from the son. It is that same line that separates the alcoholic from the burned-out businessman, the hypocrite from the dogmatic deacon, the dictator from the rising reformer, the thief from the opportunistic entrepreneur, the sin from the sinner, you from yourself.

The Bible says: "For all have sinned and fall short of the Glory of God" (Romans 3:23).

All of us have been guilty of "falling short" and missing the line. It is humanly impossible to separate the sin from the sinner, but it is heavenly possible to hate the sin and love the sinner. The Apostle John writes:

> *If we confess our sins, He is faithful and just to forgive us our sins and cleanse us from all unrighteousness* (1 John 1:9).

For a proper interpretation, you must place the words "keep on" before the verbs "confessing, forgiving and cleansing," as in "keep on confessing." If we keep on confessing, He keeps on telling us that love and grace alone can distinguish between the sin and the sinner. Christ recognized the difference when He spoke to the thief on the cross. Stephen understood it when he prayed within earshot of a young man named Saul. And with a little help from the Spirit, you too can *keep on keeping on!*

Now Saul was consenting to his [Stephen's] death.

At that time a great persecution arose against the church which was at Jerusalem; and they were all scattered throughout the regions of Judea and Samaria, except the apostles. And devout men carried Stephen to his burial, and made great lamentation over him.

As for Saul, he made havoc of the church, entering every house, and dragging off men and women, committing them to prison.

Therefore, those who were scattered went everewhere preaching the word. Then Philip went down to the city of Samaria and preached Christ to them. And the multitudes with one accord heeded the things spoken by Philip, hearing and seeing the miracles which he did. For unclean spirits, crying with a loud voice, came out of many who were possessed; and many who were paralyzed and lame were healed. And there was great joy in that city.

But there was a certain man called Simon, who previously practiced sourcery in the city and astonished the people of Samaria, claiming that he was someone great, to whom they all gave heed, from the least to the greatest, saying, "This man is the great power of God." And they heeded him because he had astonished them with his sorceries for a long time. But when they believed Philip as he preached the things concerning the kingdom of God and the name of Jesus Christ, both men and women were baptized. Then Simon himself also believed; and when he was baptized he continued with Philip, and was amazed, seeing the miracles and signs which were done.

—Acts 8:1-13

Thirteen

Unsung Fame

Simon the sorcerer was in Samaria (Acts 8:9). There was magic in the air. Abracadabra! Hocus pocus! Presto!

The crowds pressed. The people were impressed. Simon received a lot of press.

He astonished them with his sleight of hand, claiming that he was someone great, "to whom they all gave heed, from the least to the greatest, saying, 'This man is the great power of God'" (Acts 8:10).

Now you see it, now you don't!

Simon's consuming "greatness" paled pitifully compared to the consummate greatness of Philip. Simon was full of fakery. Philip was full of faith. Simon was for getting. Philip was for giving. Simon was fraudulent. Philip was forthright.

Philip preached.

Wonders wowed.

Signs surprised.

And the people believed and accepted baptism. Simon the sorcerer's greatness disappeared before his very eyes.

Now you see it, now you don't!

Pontius Pilate was full of his own greatness! At first, he undoubtedly saw Jesus as some itinerant magician who wooed the crowds with legerdemain and chicanery. But Pilate could not ignore Christ's claim to be King. His own greatness and power would be diminished if he did not consider the clamor of the crowd.

Christ claimed.

Caiaphas condemned.

Pilate pronounced the death sentence by crucifixion.

Did Pilate's power survive? No, it quickly collapsed, and an uncertain tradition has it that he killed himself on orders from Caligula, shortly after he sentenced Jesus to die.

Now you see it, now you don't!

I want to tell you about two Jims and a Jimmy, each consumed with his own greatness. The first Jim was charismatic and obsessed with power. Jim Jones moved his following to another country, and in one final triumphant act of self-absorbed "greatness," formulated a suicide pact that led them all to the slaughter.

Now you see it, now you don't!

The second Jim was possessed by money and materialism. Jim Bakker built his kingdom, under the guise of Christianity, by defrauding his flock. He has since been defrocked and served a sentence in the federal penitentiary.

Now you see it, now you don't!

The third Jimmy was dominated by sexual desire. Behind the pulpit, Jimmy Swaggart was Dr. Jekyll leading against lust. Behind the door, he was Mr. Hyde losing against lust. Little is left of his former ministry.

Now you see it, now you don't!

There is a fourth Jimmy who was consumed by God's greatness. He was possessed by grace. This Jim was a gem. He devoted himself to the J.I.M. (Jesus In Me) Club of America, located on the shores of Lake Chatauqua in New York State. The boys selected for this program paid nothing. Jimmy paid the price. My son was chosen and spent three summers under his tutelage. He was taught gospel magic and ventriloquism. He learned to lead and yearned to be led by the master and the master's Master. He left a child and returned a man. You have probably never heard of this Jimmy. His accomplishments were unsung and unheralded. Jimmy died a few years ago, but his greatness lives on in my son and a thousand other father's sons because the Son had pre-eminence in his life.

There was a fifth man. His story appears in the most widely read book ever written. An eternal bestseller. Yet this man has no claim to fame, because we don't know his name. For the sake of identification, let's call him "James." James was blind from birth, and I think you know the rest of the story:

> *He [Jesus] spat on the ground and made clay... He anointed the eyes of the blind man ... he ... washed and came back seeing* (John 9:6-7).

One thing I know [said James]: that though I was blind, now I see (John 9:25).

All because of the Man from Galilee.

The story doesn't end there. The Galilean was subsequently tortured, killed and buried for three days, when the body disappeared.

Now you see it, now you don't!

The two Marys were first to view the empty tomb (John 20:1-10). And then came Peter, John and Joe (that's me), and a multitude of pilgrims down through the centuries. While in Jerusalem, I visited two traditional burial sights: the Holy Sepulchre and the Garden Tomb.

The guide at the Garden Tomb said, "I can't tell you for certain that this is the tomb Jesus was buried in. We do know that it is outside the city walls. We do know that it is near a mount that looks like a skull. We do know that it was a rich man's tomb. We do know that the man's slab was made larger, indicating that a body other than the one for whom the tomb was intended was placed there. We do know that the tomb was empty. And after all, that's all that really counts, isn't it?"

That's the magical message of Easter. The tomb was made empty so that prophecy might be fulfilled. The tomb was made empty so that the heart might be full. The tomb was made empty so that our cup might be filled to overflowing with His life and love.

You don't see, now you do!

That's the magic of Easter.

Where there was darkness, now there is light. Where there was despair, now there is hope. Where there was sadness, now there is joy. Where there was bitterness, now there is sweetness. Where there was anxiety, now there is serenity. Where there was hate, now there is love. Where there was death, now there is life. Where there was nothing, now there is Christ.

You don't see, now you do!

That's the magic of Easter.

No other religion can make that claim. There are many proclaimed messiahs buried in Israel, but there is only one empty grave. No other religion can make that claim. No other religion can sing:

> *Up from the grave He arose,*
> *With a mighty triumph o'er His foes.*
> *He arose a victor from the dark domain,*
> *And He lives forever with His saints to reign.*
> *He arose! He arose! Hallelujah!*
> *Christ arose!*

—Robert Lowry

You don't see, now you do!

That's the magic of Easter.

For those without Christ, there is darkness at the end of the tunnel, while the redeemed have already broken forth into everlasting light. No other religion can make that claim. No other religion can sing:

> *Let us rejoice, the fight is won,*
> *Darkness is conquered, death undone,*
> *Life triumphant! Alleluia!*

—Percy Dearmer

You don't see, now you do!

That's the magic of Easter.

Leaders and followers of other faiths are still seeking Nirvana and coming up with nothing, while Christ's followers have sought and found everything because of one simple, uncomplicated, amazing act of grace. No other religion can make that claim. No other religion can sing:

> *Amazing grace! How sweet the sound,*
> *That saved a wretch like me!*
> *I once was lost, but now am found,*
> *Was blind, but now I see.*
>
> —John Newton

You don't see, now you do!

That's the magic of Easter, and the magic is that there is really no magic at all.

Oh, by the way, my middle name is James.

I didn't see, now I do!

And when Simon saw that through the laying on of the apostles' hands the Holy Spirit was given, he offered them money, saying, "Give me this power also, that anyone on whom I lay hands may receive the Holy Spirit."

But Peter said to him, "Your money perish with you, because you thought that the gift of God could be purchased with money! You have neither part nor portion in this matter, for your heart is not right in the sight of God. Repent therefore of this your wickedness, and pray God if perhaps the thought of your heart may be forgiven you."

—*Acts 8:18-22*

Fourteen

Priceless Gift

Simon the sorcerer was witnessing a power that was beyond his comprehension. The lame man leaped without levitation. "How did you do it?" Simon asked. The leper was cleansed right before his very eyes. "I've never seen that one before!" he cried. The split personality was made whole without first being cut in half. "That one is not in my bag of tricks. I want some of your gospel magic," Simon pleaded.

Simon believed. He was baptized, but was baffled because he had not received the Holy Spirit. Then came the *pièce de résistance*, the ultimate divination, the trick to end all tricks. Then came Peter and John:

> *Who, when they had come down, prayed for them that they might receive the Holy Spirit. For as yet He had fallen upon none of them. They had only been*

baptized in the name of the Lord Jesus. Then they laid hands on them and they received the Holy Spirit (Acts 8:15-17).

It was the second of many blessings that were yet to come. It was a second work of grace, but only the beginning of a life full of grace. It was the second filling of a cup that would be filling and spilling over and over again.

Simon saw smiles where there had been no smiles. Simon felt serenity where there had been no serenity. Simon experienced spirit where there had been no spirit. "The other tricks were good, but this one was great!" he exclaimed. "How did you do it? No, better yet, I'll buy the trick from you." He continued, saying: "'Give me this power also, that anyone on whom I lay hands may receive the Holy Spirit.' But Peter said to him, 'Your money perish with you, because you thought the gift of God could be purchased with money!'" (Acts 8:19-20).

Simon the sorcerer was a profiteer. Peter the rock was a prophet-seer. One saw the gospel as magic to be bought. The other saw the gospel as grace to be wrought.

Simon the sorcerer thought the formula for gospel magic, "Now you see it, now you don't," had to be taught, bought and sought. But Peter the rock knew that, with gospel grace, there are no strings attached.

It can't be taught. *Either you know it or you don't.*
It can't be bought. *Either you take it or you don't.*
It can't be sought. *Either you deserve it or you don't.*
And, in the case of gospel grace, you don't deserve it.
Either you know it or you don't.

My son Robby, 10 years old, was returning home from J.I.M. camp. He sat on the floor, in the middle of the airport, performing magic tricks he had learned that summer. A crowd gathered. At the conclusion of one particular trick, a curious onlooker said, "How did you do that, son?" Robby's eyes playfully darted from person to person, finally landing on the man who asked the question. In a voice a little louder than a whisper, he said, "Can you keep a secret, mister?" "I certainly can," said the man. The crowd drew closer, their necks strained with anticipation. There was a long, dramatic pause. Finally, Robby giggled and shouted, "So can I, mister!" The crowd laughed, and in that moment, Robby revealed the first cardinal rule of magic: "You have to keep the secret a secret."

Gospel magic is concealing. Gospel grace is revealing. God can't keep a secret. It is cried from the cross. It is trumpeted from the tomb. It is shouted from the Scriptures. It is no secret what God can do. Either you know it or you don't.

He who has ears to hear, let him hear! (Matthew 11:15).

Either you take it or you don't.

Both my sons are now budding magicians, and you think they can share? Nooooo! To each his own. Gospel magic is an expensive craft, and who pays the price? Good old dad.

Upon arriving home from the airport, Robby plopped himself on the living room floor and proceeded to show us the new tricks in his repertoire. After one such trick, I naively asked, "How did you do that?" You already know the rest of the story. Then Robby went on to reveal the second cardinal rule of magic: "You have to buy the trick before you can learn the secret, Dad," he said. "But I did buy the trick, son," I said. "No, Dad," he said. "You don't understand. You bought the trick for me, not for you."

Gospel magic is exclusive. Gospel grace is inclusive. It is available for the taking. Jesus has already paid the price for his children. Either you take it or you don't.

He who has ears to hear, let him hear.

Either you deserve it or you don't.

My boys were not always on the deserving end. On the other hand, the more proficient they became in manipulating the tricks they had, the more deserving they became of moving on to the next level.

And speaking of manipulation, I was most vulnerable at bedtime when listening to their prayers.

God bless Mommy
God bless Daddy
God bless … etc.
Help me to be a good boy
And help me get that trick I really want.
Amen.

How can you resist those angelic faces tucked in at the end of a day? They don't deserve it, but they are going to get it anyway.

The third cardinal rule of gospel magic is: "You move up to the next level of skill by mastery." The more proficient you become, the more deserving you become. The more deserving you become, the greater the price.

Gospel magic is manipulated. Gospel grace is manifested. It is not obscure. It is obvious. It is not disguised. It is displayed. It is not purchased. It is possessed. You don't deserve it, but you get it anyway.

He who has ears to hear, let him hear.

Oh, by the way, my son's best trick is making my money disappear. Come to think of it, there are others who know that trick, too. *And I still don't know how they do it!*

[Peter said,] "Repent therefore of this your wickedness, and pray God if perhaps the thought of your heart may be forgiven you. For I see that you are poisoned by bitterness and bound by iniquity."

Then Simon answered and said, "Pray to the Lord for me, that none of the things which you have spoken may come upon me."

So when they had testified and preached the word of the Lord, they returned to Jerusalem, preaching the gospel in many villages of the Samaritans.

—Acts 8:22-25

Fifteen

Bitter Sweetness

Peter preached without pulling punches (Acts 8:22-23).
Poisoned by bitterness.
Repent your wickedness!
Pray for forgiveness.
Simon the sorcerer was a persistent fellow.

> *Pray to the Lord for me, that none of the things you*
> *have spoken may come upon me* (Acts 8:24).

This section in the Scriptures concludes with a cliff-hanger. There is a great void between verses 24 and 25. Did Simon the sorcerer repent and pray? The Bible writers often leave us with a teaser, giving us just enough to whet the appetite, just enough to arouse our curiosity, just enough to make us think. And besides, even the most brilliant among us cannot grasp or comprehend the omniscience of God.

(I've been in some circles where one or two think they can.) John wrote ...

> *And there are also many other things that Jesus did, which if they were written one by one, I suppose that even the world itself could not contain the books that would be written. Amen* (John 21:25).

Amen! What Jesus said and did represents but one meager sentence in God's eternal encyclopedia of knowledge—just enough to exercise our faith ... and I get plenty of exercise.

I grew up in the era of movie theater serials. Every episode ended with a cliffhanger similar to the following:

Hopalong Cassidy (wearing a white hat) is precariously perched on the edge of a precipice. The music crescendos as the bad guy (wearing a black hat) peers down the barrel of a six shooter and growls villainously, "This is the last mountain you'll ever climb, Hoppy!" The camera fades to black and the words, "To be continued next week," appear anti-climactically upon the screen. Hopalong's predicament was the topic of conversation all week long, and I could hardly wait until the next Saturday matinee when I would finally learn the fate of my hero.

And I can hardly wait until heaven, when I will find the answers to my fretful and fateful questions. And one of those questions will be, "Was Simon the sorcerer's life a bittersweet experience? Did he repent? Was he forgiven?" If so, I will meet him and we will "talk story" together, because I will have found another kindred spirit.

Bitterness of the soul will enhance our enjoyment when

we finally taste the sweetness of the Spirit. The devil tempts us continually as he dangles a bitter carrot of lust and evil cloaked in sweetness.

We see …

We seek …

We succumb.

And the sweetness turns sour until the difference between the two is indistinguishable. It is only when we begin to savor the sweetness of the Savior, through the indwelling presence of His Spirit, that we can truly triumph over all earthly barriers.

Christianity is not a present-tense panacea. It is a future-tense phenomenon. Jesus didn't promise us a rose garden. There are no magic solutions to our problems. Whether we live above the poverty level or below it, there will always be bills to pay. Inflation will continue to grow as your pocketbook shrinks. Mortgage payments will likely dog you all the days of your life. Insurance premiums will rise along with your blood pressure. Baldness will still be the plague of vain men. Chocolate will still contain calories. And there will always be suffering, sadness and sorrow in this life.

Life in the present tense is at worst a bitter experience and at best a bittersweet process. Oh yes, we find help to cope with the trials and tribulations that are sure to be ours even after a Spirit-filled intervention.

God is our refuge and strength, a very present help in trouble (Psalm 45:1).

Let us therefore come boldly to the throne of grace,

that we may obtain mercy and find grace to help in time of need (Hebrews 4:16).

But more important, we find hope to cope with present circumstances because our future is secure.

And not only that, but we also glory in tribulations, knowing that tribulation produces perseverance; and perseverance, character; and character, hope. Now hope does not disappoint, because the love of God has been poured out in our hearts by the Holy Spirit who was given to us (Romans 5:3-5).

Blessed be the God and Father of our Lord Jesus Christ, who according to His abundant mercy has begotten us again to a living hope through the resurrection of Jesus Christ from the dead (1 Peter 1:3-4).

Greatness will come when we find the right mix. I heard the story somewhere about a little girl who was fixing herself a glass of lemonade. Her father was watching as she slowly and methodically put five heaping tablespoons of sugar into the lemonade. He said, "Honey, don't you think the lemonade will be too sweet?" "No, Daddy," she responded, "not if you don't stir it."

Some days you will be in the rose garden and other days in the lemon grove. You have two choices in life:

Smell and suffer or smile and …

Stir!

Now an angel of the Lord spoke to Philip, saying, "Arise and go toward the south along the road which goes down from Jerusalem to Gaza." This is desert. So he arose and went. And behold, a man of Ethiopia, a eunuch of great authority under Candace the queen of the Ethiopians, who had charge of all her treasury, and had come to Jerusalem to worship, was returning. And sitting in his chariot, he was reading Isaiah the prophet. Then the Spirit said to Philip, "Go near and overtake this chariot."

So Philip ran to him, and heard him reading the prophet Isaiah, and said, "Do you understand what you are reading?"

And he said, "How can I, unless someone guides me?" And he asked Philip to come up and sit with him. The place in the Scripture which he read was this:

"He was led as a sheep to the slaughter;
And as a lamb before it's shearer is silent,
So He opened not His mouth.
In His humiliation His justice was taken away,
And who will declare His generation?
For His life is taken from the earth."

So the eunuch answered Philip and said, "I ask you, of whom does the prophet say this, of himself or of some other man?" Then Philip opened his mouth, and beginning at this Scripture, preached Jesus to him. Now as they went down the road, they came to some water. And the eunuch said, "See, here is water. What hinders me from being baptized?"

Then Philip said, "If you believe with all your heart, you may."

And he answered and said, "I believe that Jesus Christ is the Son of God."

—Acts 8:26-37

Sixteen

Comings and Goings

The message rang out …
The news travelled …
The Word spread.

Jesus was no pew potato, not by any stretch of the imagination. His comings and goings are well-documented as an integral part of His life and ministry. There is nothing status quo about the gospel. Jesus was constantly on the move, leaving joy in His wake. Good news cries out to be shared. Bad news travels fast, but good news travels even faster because it is contagious. That's why the Bible is the leading bestseller of all time. The good news Jesus shared was especially contagious because it had that something …

Extra! Extra! Read all about it!

WEDDING PARTY WINES UP!

Something extraordinary took place in the little town of

Cana last evening. There was a wedding party, and they ran out of wine quite early. It was reported that Mary, the mother of a man named Jesus, asked her Son to do something about it. He resisted, saying something strange: "My hour has not yet come." Mary wouldn't take no for an answer, and finally Jesus said, "Fill the waterpots with water." Eyewitnesses concur that water went into the six waterpots. When the master of the feast tasted the water, he said to the bridegroom, "You have kept the good wine until now." The bridegroom was perplexed, insisting that the good wine was put out first, according to custom (John 2:1-11). Yet everyone present agreed this was the best wine they had ever tasted. This was one party that "wined up before it wined down" because it had that something ...

Extra! Extra! Read all about it!
MIRACLE MUD SWAMPS GALILEE!

A new craze is sweeping across Galilee. It is reported that this man called Jesus has discovered a new cure for blindness and other maladies of the eye. Reputable eyewitnesses say he prepared a mudpack and placed it over the eyes of a man who had been blind since birth (John 9:1-41). The news has spread, and many people are seen in and around Capernaum sporting mudpacks. It has become a real eyesore in the city. It appears that the mudpack will only work if Jesus applies it because it has that something ...

Extra! Extra! Read all about it!
TEN LEPERS LEAPING!

It was a sight to behold. Ten lepers leaping with joy after they had been cleansed by the "miracle worker." Nine disappeared and one, a Samaritan, remaining behind reported, "I can't believe that He would touch me, a foreigner, one despised by the Jews. Now there are toes where there were none. I can dance again. He truly is the Son of God!" (Luke 17:11-19). This reporter has covered some strange stories in his day but none quite like this. What's next?

Extra! Extra! Read all about it!

DEATH DEFYING ACT!

There is great controversy in Israel these days. Some say that Jesus' body was stolen from the grave and buried elsewhere. Many claim that He was resurrected from the dead on the third day, and many have actually sighted Him. One group swears they saw Him walk through a door without opening it. Two say they walked with Him on the road to Emmaus, and one doubter became a believer saying, "I touched the nailprint in His hands." Peter, one of His disciples, preaches a living Christ and testifies that "His signs and wonders may be done through me." Supernatural feats seem to continue even after Jesus' death. Two men have reported that they personally escorted Peter to Joppa and the house of Dorcas, where the owner's body lay in the upper room awaiting burial. "Peter entered the room, and a few minutes later reappeared with Dorcas, presenting her alive," they said (Acts 9:36-42). Peter has become very popular, and people are coming from near and far to see him perform his "death-defying acts."

Extra! Extra! Read all about it!

ETHIOPIAN RECEIVES HEART TRANSPLANT!

A eunuch from Ethiopia became the latest recipient of

a new heart. In an interview this morning he said, "I was sitting alone in my chariot trying to understand the Scriptures, when a man called Philip stopped by and witnessed to me, preaching Jesus Christ. I was really searching and wanted to know why I couldn't know this Christ personally. Philip made it so simple, saying, 'If you believe with all your heart, you may.' My heart leaped within me when I heard this good news, and I said I believe that Jesus Christ is the Son of God (Acts 8:26-40). I can give you no scientific explanation for what has happened to me. Before my heart was filled with sadness, and now it is overflowing with joy. Before my heart was empty, and now it is full. Then it was broken, and now it is new!"

Philip continues to preach in all the cities, and spiritual heart transplants are taking place in record numbers—including my own. I have been a reporter for many years and must confess that I have never covered a story that is so persuasive.

Extra! Extra! Read all about it!

You have heard the Good News. Will your name be included in God's book: The Lamb's Book of Life? Great grace is available to you. Receive it and find your name in the …

HEAVENLY HEADLINES!

Part 3

Great Joy

"And there was great joy in that city" (Acts 8:8).

Spontaneous Spiritual Communion

Spontaneous spiritual communion is when your cup of joy is full and running over. My favorite Sunday school chorus is:

> *Running over, running over.*
> *My cup is full and running over.*
> *Since the Lord saved me,*
> *I'm as happy as can be.*
> *My cup is full and running over.*

The verse brings back memories of happy times in the midst of harrowing ones. Sunday school was a haven from the storm of my father's alcoholism, which hovered about me continuously during my childhood and adolescent years. Sunday school was a sanctuary from the tempest that tossed me, a shelter from the turbulence that raged within. That chorus was and is a reminder of my joy and salvation.

The Psalmist understood:

> *Yea, though I walk through the valley of the shadow*
> *of death, I will fear no evil; for You are with me; Your*
> *rod and Your staff, they comfort me. You prepare a*

table before me in the presence of my enemies; You anoint my head with oil; my cup runs over. Surely goodness and mercy shall follow me all the days of my life; and I will dwell in the house of the LORD forever (Psalm 23:4-6).

The Apostle Paul understood. He was in prison facing persecution and death when he wrote:

Rejoice in the Lord always. Again I will say, rejoice! (Philippians 4:4).

Jesus understands. It was during the most difficult time of His life when …

… He took the cup, and gave thanks, and gave it to them saying, "Drink from it, all of you. For this is My blood of the new covenant, which is shed for many for the remission of sins. But I say to you, I will not drink of this fruit of the vine from now on until that day when I drink it new with you in My Father's kingdom" (Matthew 26:27-29).

The happiest person I know understands. He spent 10 years in a communist concentration camp because of his faith. During that time, his oldest son was murdered because of his faith. Not long after tasting freedom, his wife died. Soon after that, his second son was paralyzed from the waist down in an automobile accident. I visited with them in the hospital, and he ministered to me. After suffering all of this, his cup is still full and running over. Brigadier Josef Korbel (R) is a joy to behold. He helped me to understand that great joy is not only spontaneous, it's contagious!

As for Saul, he made havoc of the church, entering every house, and dragging off men and women, committing them to prison. …

As he journeyed he came near Damascus, and suddenly a light shone around him from heaven. Then he fell to the ground, and heard a voice saying to him, "Saul, Saul, why are you persecuting Me?"

And he said, "Who are You, Lord?"

Then the Lord said, "I am Jesus, whom you are persecuting. It is hard for you to kick against the goads."

… Then Saul arose from the ground, and when his eyes were opened he saw no one. But they led him by the hand and brought him into Damascus. And he was three days without sight, and neither ate nor drank.

Now there was a certain disciple at Damascus named Ananias; and to him the Lord said in a vision, "Ananias."

And he said, "Here I am, Lord."

So the Lord said to him, "Arise and go to the street called Straight, and inquire at the house of Judas for one called Saul of Tarsus, for behold, he is praying. And in a vision he has seen a man named Ananias coming in and putting his hand on him, so that he might receive his sight."

Then Ananias answered, "Lord, I have heard from many about this man, how much harm he has done to Your saints in Jerusalem. And here he has authority from the chief priests to bind all who call on Your name."

But the Lord said to him, "Go, for he is a chosen vessel of Mine to bear My name before Gentiles, kings, and the children of Israel. For I will show him how many things he must suffer for My name's sake."

And Ananias went his way and entered the house; and laying his hands on him he said, "Brother Saul, the Lord Jesus who appeared to you on the road as you came, has sent me that you may receive your sight and be filled with the Holy Spirit." Immediately there fell from his eyes something like scales, and he received his sight at once; and he arose and was baptized. —Acts 8:3; 9:3-5, 8-18

Seventeen

Blindsight

Saul made havoc.

Saul spread hate.

Saul raised hell as the legions of evil were summoned for support.

He was bitter, brazen and blind. He was driven by blind fury, blind faith, blind ambition until God gave him blindsight. Being without, he was forced to look within. He had no choice but to concentrate on the Light. He made the choice to consecrate his life.

> *Immediately there fell from his eyes something like scales, and he received his sight at once; and he arose and was baptized* (Acts 9:18).

Why was Saul so resentful and revenge-full? Because he was human, just like you and me. We know that he was blind to many of his shortcomings, just like you and me. We know that he was blaming everyone and everything else for his problems, just like you and I do. We know he had a "thorn in his flesh," just like you and I do. We don't know what his "thorn" was, but we should know what our own is.

Let me get right to the point!

Thorns come in many shapes and sizes. Their prick is pervasive, reaching into every crevice of the mind, body and spirit. Thorns constantly remind us that the proverbial "bed of roses" is not without its Gethsemane. Thorns are an integral part of the garden. They were present at Gethsemane and Golgotha. And Paul too was plagued with them as we are today. A crown without thorns has no eternal value. A crown without thorns has no lasting power. A crown without thorns has no ongoing future. Thorns help us keep our life mission in perspective. They remind us that there is always a price to pay. They help us get the point!

Saul was so angry he couldn't see straight. He was staying on a street called Straight when he finally straightened up and got the point!

Paul made harmony.

Paul spread happiness.

Paul raised heaven as the Spirit of God entered and filled his soul with Glory.

He raised his sights and the sight of others by giving them a clear and accessible view of Heaven. Instead of looking out, he was looking up. Blindsight helps us get the point.

It was a long time before I understood why we close our eyes to pray. Some saint once told me, "You can see better with your eyes closed." "Sure," I thought and proceeded blindly on life's journey with my eyes wide open. Oh, there would be a blink now and then, but the blink quickly turned to blank, and I continued unhappily on my way, looking out for number one. I worried about what others said and saw, instead of worrying about what Jesus said and saw. I really believed that "they" were the enemy. It took a major crisis for me to realize that "they are us." I finally closed my eyes and got the point!

A pilot must have 20/20 vision. There are some who have the uncanny ability to see deep into the horizon and spot the enemy approaching before anyone else. They tell me that this is the difference between a good fighter pilot and a great fighter pilot. But even the great ones need help on occasion. Even the great ones cannot see beyond the horizon. Even they cannot see in the blackness of night. They are forced to rely on their instrumentation for guidance. They must "look within" the cockpit and focus on the light panel.

Our vision is limited without, but if we look within, we can see the enemy approaching. If we focus on the Light, we can see forever. This is the difference between a good person and a great person, a good life and a great life, one who missed the point and one who got the point!

A little boy stood in front of a supermarket with a basket full of newborn puppies and a sign reading, "Puppies for sale! $5.00 each." Several weeks later the boy was still standing there, but the sign had been changed to read, "Puppies for sale! $25.00 each." A man who had seen the first sign stopped and said, "I don't understand. Why have the puppies suddenly increased in value?" The little boy answered confidently, "Well, you see mister, now their eyes are open."

When your eyes are finally opened spiritually, life will take on great value. And if you look within, your life will be filled with great joy.

Get the point?

Then he said to them, "You know how unlawful it is for a Jewish man to keep company with or go to one of another nation. But God has shown me that I should not call any man common or unclean. Therefore I came without objection as soon as I was sent for. I ask, then, for what reason have you sent for me?"

So Cornelius said, "Four days ago I was fasting until this hour; and at the ninth hour I prayed in my house, and behold, a man stood before me in bright clothing, and said, 'Cornelius, your prayer has been heard, and your alms are remembered in the sight of God. Send therefore to Joppa and call Simon here, whose surname is Peter. He is lodging in the house of Simon, a tanner, by the sea. When he comes, he will speak to you.' So I sent to you immediately, and you have done well to come. Now therefore, we are all present before God, to hear all the things commanded you by God."

Then Peter opened his mouth and said: "In truth I perceive that God shows no partiality. But in every nation whoever fears Him and works righteousness is accepted by Him. The word which God sent to the children of Israel, preaching peace through Jesus Christ—He is Lord of all."

—Acts 10:28-36

Eighteen

Same Difference

Perceived differences between Jews and Gentiles divided the land. Their world was split by prejudice and dissension. Anyone not a Jew was a Gentile and considered heathen. Jews were "chosen," and Gentiles were "frozen" out. Dogma gripped the Promised Land.

Jesus wanted to capture a different picture through a new lens. His portfolio reveals a masterpiece of color and contrast.

His first snapshot is a self-portrait, showing Jesus the Jew speaking to a Samaritan. In 720 B.C., the Assyrians invaded Samaria and began to inter-marry. William Barclay tells us, "They committed what to the Jews was an unforgivable crime. They lost their racial purity. In a strict Jewish household, even to this day, if a son or daughter marries a Gentile, his or her funeral service is carried out. Such a person is dead in the eyes of orthodox Judaism." Jesus was speaking to a Samaritan.

Get the picture?

His second snapshot is another self-portrait, showing Jesus the rabbi speaking to a woman. Once again, Barclay tells us that, "The strict rabbis forbade a rabbi to greet a woman in public. A rabbi might not even speak to his own wife or daughter or sister in public. There were even Pharisees who were called the bruised and bleeding Pharisees because they shut their eyes when they saw a woman on the street and so walked into walls and houses!" A rabbi seen speaking to a woman in public risked ruining his reputation, yet Jesus spoke to this woman.

Get the picture?

His third snapshot in the series is another self-portrait, showing Jesus the man speaking to a woman of questionable character. She had four husbands, and the man she was living with was not her husband. No decent man would be seen speaking to a woman of such ill repute. Jesus was speaking to a fallen woman.

Get the picture?

In another setting, Pentecost had passed. Peter was hungry as he climbed the rooftop to pray. With a deft touch, the Master photographer created yet another heavenly portrait depicting a dieter's dilemma, an epicurean delight, a gourmet delicatessen.

All were forbidden. A tablecloth descended, filled with gastronomical fare—foreign to the Jewish palate and forbidden by Hebrew law. Entrées included curried camel, stewed sea urchin, broiled buzzard, barbecued bat, cashewed cricket, marinated mole, and even grilled gecko. The list of common and unclean delicacies goes on *ad nauseam* in Leviticus 2.

I was surprised to find "gecko" on Moses' Levitical list. For some time, I lived in Hawaii, where the gecko is enshrined on t-shirts and posters. These little lizards are revered because they eat roaches, cane spiders, centipedes and every manner of crawling things. They are treated with respect and have full, free reign of the house. But green gecko pu-pu's on my platter? Not on your life!

Peter had a point. Kosher it wasn't. Common it was. God was going to prove His point. Cleansed it was. Commanded it was:

> *Rise, Peter; kill and eat ... what God has cleansed you must not call common* (Acts 10:13, 15).

God didn't make his point once or twice. God made his point three times, and it was made very clear when Peter kept his appointment with Cornelius the centurion and his Gentile relatives and friends.

The lens focused:

> *You know how unlawful it is for a Jewish man to keep company with or to go to one of another nation. But God has shown me that I should not call any man common or unclean* (Acts 10:28).

The camera clicked:

> *In truth I perceive that God shows no partiality* (Acts 10:34).

The bulb flashed:

> *The word which God sent to the children of Israel,*
> *preaching peace through Jesus Christ—He is Lord*
> *of all* (Acts 10:36).

Peter got the picture!

The gecko and Gentile had something in common. Although "common," they were clean. They were created by the same God that created Peter. With one setting of the shutter, Jesus portrays a picture of peace. In one shoot, our Lord unveils a portrait of His plan. In a simple scene, God poses His purpose, and Peter is poised to change the course of mankind. Jew or Gentile? In God's eyes, it's the same difference.

Peter had to adapt before he could adopt. Peter had to acquiesce before he could accelerate. Peter had to adjust before he could advance. The Christian movement was freeze-framed until Peter got the picture. It was freeze-framed until Luther got the picture. Christianity was freeze-framed until Booth got the picture. It was freeze-framed until Graham got the picture. Christianity was freeze-framed until I and a host of other unknown soldiers down through the centuries got the picture.

Great joy is only a snapshot away.

Get the picture?

Now the apostles and brethren who were in Judea heard that the Gentiles had also received the word of God. And when Peter came up to Jerusalem, those of the circumcision contended with him, saying, "You went in to uncircumcised men and ate with them!" …

"If therefore God gave them the same gift as He gave us when we believed on the Lord Jesus Christ, who was I that I could withstand God?"

When they heard these things they became silent; and they glorified God, saying, "Then God has also granted to the Gentiles repentance to life."

—Acts 11:1-3, 17-18

Nineteen

Out Is In

Peter's new diet distressed his brethren greatly. Can you picture their skewed faces as they cried out, "You what?" "You went in to uncircumcised men and ate with them!" (Acts 11:3).

They were obviously reacting both to the cuisine and the company. I remember trying to explain the Alaska culinary experience to my children when they were small. I went into great detail, describing seal steak and squid smothered in seaweed and seasoned with salmon eggs. Their reaction was as different as their personalities. Guy punctuated my patter with, "Ugh! Yuk! Ahh!" And his concluding expletive was, "Barf in a bucket," one of the more picturesque colloquialisms of his generation.

On the other hand, Rob, the more adventurous one, listened intently, never uttering a sound. When I had finished, he bellowed, "Far out, Dad!"

They were obviously reacting to the cuisine and knew nothing about the company. Peter continued:

> *If therefore God gave them the same gift as He gave us when we believed on the Lord Jesus Christ, who was I that I could withstand God?* (Acts 11:17).

They sat silently. They listened intently. They exclaimed enthusiastically, "Far out, Peter!" which is a modern translation of, "Then God has also granted to the Gentiles repentance to life" (Acts 11:18).

In both instances, the place was far away and the food was foreign. But the fellowship was "far out!" And the message hasn't changed over two millennia. The same friend … the same Father … the same fellowship.

I can't think of a more descriptive phrase for this phenomenon than, far out!

I think a language lesson is appropriate at this point, especially for those of us belonging to the geriatric generation (anyone over 30).

Spaced out: In another world mentally and emotionally, generally as a result of drugs. You might say this person is doing it the "high way."

Way out: Closely related to the expression, "out in left field." Strange, different, eccentric or free-spirited. You might say this person is doing it the "my way."

Far out: In the purest sense, a derivative of the theological concept, "omnipresent." Far is near. Out is in. Infinite is accessible. Creation is within. God is personal. Scattered is together. You might say this person is doing it the "Thy way."

My kids and I were discussing a childhood friend who strayed from the path and decided to do it "my way." She got on a fast track and joined the counter-culture. Experimentation with drugs, sex and alcohol led her to the "high way." The boys had written her off. But God hadn't. She's a brand new person now and doing it "Thy way." My kids' response was, "Far out!" In other words, she had a close encounter of the infinite kind.

My kids would say that Jesus living within is a "far out" experience. Through Christ we are "scattered together." There are many directions but only *one way!*

Unity emerges from diversity. Paul understood this principle well when he prayed:

> ... *that Christ may dwell in your hearts through faith; that you, being rooted and grounded in love, may be able to comprehend with all the saints what is the width and length and depth and height—to know the love of Christ which passes knowledge; that you may be filled with all the fullness of God* (Ephesians 3:17-19).

Far is near when measured by the Creator. How else could an infinite God be so far away and yet so close? You can't get closer than within. His omnipresent infilling is the glue that binds us together in a way incomprehensible to the uninitiated. That's why the first century Church was so powerful, its leaders so prolific, its converts so plentiful.

Believers were scattered, going in separate directions, practicing diverse lifestyles and cultures, yet united together by one common purpose. There was a great "joy inexpressible and full of glory" (1 Peter 1:8) that joined them together.

*Now those who were scattered ... traveled ... far ...
preaching the Lord Jesus. And the hand of the Lord
was with them, and a great number believed and
turned to the Lord* (Acts 11:19-21).

Although scattered, they were joined by a common bond
and a common name ...

*... and the disciples were first called Christians in
Antioch* (Acts 11:26).

Their great joy and fellowship remains accessible today.

*Lord, I cannot find my way out
Until Thou hast found Thy way in.
Amen.*

If you pray this prayer, you, too, will find that His way is ...

far out!

Then the disciples, each according to his ability, determined to send relief to the brethren dwelling in Judea.

—Acts 11:29

Twenty

Bound and Determined

We are faced with two options in life: to be bound and defeated or bound and determined.

We are born with our limitations.

One child was born in Egypt, into a slave nation. He was born a male when male babies were being murdered. By some standards he was an abandoned child. He was adopted into a single-parent home. He was a victim of prejudice. He grew up to lead the Hebrews from slavery to freedom.

Another was raised in Nazareth ("Can any good thing come out of Nazareth?" people wondered). His parents were not married. Because of His birth, all male babies under the age of three were sought out and murdered. He was homeless for a time: "But the Son of Man has nowhere to lay His head" (Matthew 8:20). He was abandoned by many. He was a victim of prejudice. He would grow up to die that the world might have eternal life.

Another child was born in Georgia into the cesspool of segregation. He was born black. He was abused and abandoned by society. He was a victim of prejudice. He would grow up to rekindle the American dream of "liberty and justice for all."

Limitations are not barriers. They are hurdles to be catapulted, fences to be climbed and mountains to be conquered. We are bound by our ability.

The first child, highly educated, was bound by his slowness of speech. His brother became his spokesman and press secretary. He was a born leader, but there were not enough hours in the day to lead alone. His father-in-law became his counselor, advising:

> Both you and these people who are with you will
> surely wear yourselves out. For this thing is too much
> for you; you are not able to perform it by yourself.
> Listen to my voice; I will give you counsel ... You
> shall select from all the people able men, such as fear
> God ... and place such over them to be rulers
> (Exodus 18:18, 19, 21).

The second child, the Son of God, was bound by His humanity. He could only be in one place at one time, offering hope and healing for the body, mind and spirit. He could not do it alone so He empowered eleven others, saying:

> All authority has been given to Me in heaven and on
> earth. Go, therefore and make disciples of all the na-
> tions, baptizing them in the name of the Father and
> of the Son and of the Holy Spirit, teaching them to

observe all things that I have commanded you; and
lo, I am with you always, even to the end of the age
(Matthew 28:18-21).

The third child, intelligent and eloquent, was bound by his sense of purpose and direction. Role models, teachers and ministers pointed him down the right path that led to a Nobel Peace Prize. In the process, he received a crown of gold. He carried a torch along the path of righteousness and lit the flame in others because he would be unable to fulfill his Great Commission alone. His acts of civil disobedience inspired a nation to practice its ideals.

Peace I leave with you, My peace I give to you; not as
the world gives do I give to you. Let not your heart
be troubled, neither let it be afraid (John 14:27).

We cannot do it alone. This was the lesson the disciples first learned at Pentecost!

Then the disciples, each according to his ability, de-
termined to send relief to the brethren dwelling in
Judea (Acts 11:29).

We cannot do it overnight.

We are loosed by our vision.

Moses had the ability, but it took him 80 years to get the vision. And it took something very dramatic indeed—a burning bush, a slithering snake, a leprous limb.

These signs gave Moses a 20/20 visionary look beyond the bondage of his people. He was loosened up and set free so that the people might be set free and become heaven-bound.

Jesus was a visionary from the very beginning. It took His disciples three years to get the vision. And it took something very dramatic indeed—a crucifixion, a resurrection, a sanctification.

These significant events gave the disciples a 20/20 visionary look beyond the grip of Jesus' death. They were loosened up and set free so that people everywhere might be set free and become heaven-bound.

Dr. Martin Luther King caught the vision from the words of the Bible. And it took something very dramatic indeed— a charred cross, a blown building, a massive march.

These unfortunate circumstances gave him a 20/20 visionary look beyond the walls of separation. Dr. King was loosened and set free so that the people divided by those oppressive walls might be set free and become heaven-bound.

As disciples we must loosen up and catch God's vision. But it doesn't stop there because we must then be ...

Stretched by our determination.

Moses was stretched to the limit through pestilence and petulance as he determined to fulfill God's providential plan.

Martin was stretched to the limit through bias and bigotry, as he determined to fulfill God's providential plan.

We too can be stretched to the limit because ...

We are empowered by His presence.

Moses and Martin were not perfect, but they were driven by the same holy source. Moses and Martin were able to say, "I have seen the promised land." The Messiah promised:

*In My Father's house are many mansions; if it were
not so I would have told you. I go to prepare a place
for you. And if I go and prepare a place for you, I
will come again and receive you to Myself; that where
I am, there you may be also* (John 14:2-3).

This same divine promise brings great joy as it unbinds
and propels me *Heaven bound!*

I don't know about you, but when St. Peter opens those
legendary gates I'm going to be ...

Spellbound!

And when Herod was about to bring him out, that night Peter was sleeping, bound with two chains between two soldiers; and the guards before the door were keeping the prison. Now behold, an angel of the Lord stood by him, and a light shone in the prison; and he struck Peter on the side and raised him up saying, "Arise quickly!" And his chains fell off his hands. Then the angel said to him, "Gird yourself and tie on your sandals"; and so he did. And he said to him, "Put on your garment and follow me." So he went out and followed him, and did not know that what was done by the angel was real, but thought he was seeing a vision. When they were past the first and the second guard posts, they came to the iron gate that leads to the city, which opened to them of its own accord; and they went out and went down one street, and immediately the angel departed from him.

And when Peter had come to himself, he said, "Now I know for certain that the Lord has sent His angel, and has delivered me from the hand of Herod and from all the expectation of the Jewish people."

So, when he had considered this, he came to the house of Mary, the mother of John whose surname was Mark, where many were gathered together praying.

—Acts 12:6-12

Twenty-One

Inside Out

James, the brother of John, was executed by the sword. When Herod saw how much this pleased the religious authorities of his day, he seized Peter and threw him into prison to await the same fate.

> And when Herod was about to bring him out, that night Peter was sleeping, bound with two chains between two soldiers; and the guards before the door were keeping the prison (Acts 12:6).

The angel stood. The angel struck. The angel said, "'Arise quickly!' And his chains fell off his hands" (Acts 12:7b).

Peter was perplexed. "Is this for real?" Peter thought. "Am I seeing things?" he wondered. "Maybe this is a dream," he muttered as he followed the angel.

> When they were past the first and the second guard posts, they came to the iron gate that leads to the city,

> *which opened to them of its own accord; and they*
> *went out and went down one street, and immediately*
> *the angel departed from him* (Acts 12:10).

His eyes opened.

His head cleared.

His thoughts focused.

> *And when Peter had come to himself, he said, "Now I*
> *know for certain that the Lord has sent his angel,*
> *and has delivered me from ... Herod and from all the*
> *expectations of the Jewish people"* (Acts 12:11).

When Peter had come to himself, he went to the house
of Mary and knocked. Rhoda, shocked, was beside herself.
The others, astonished, were inside themselves. Peter was
left alone outside himself.

> *But motioning to them with his hand to keep silent,*
> *he declared to them how the Lord had brought him*
> *out of the prison. And he said, "Go, tell these things*
> *to James and to the brethren"* (Acts 12:17).

The Lord brought Peter from the inside of prison to the
outside so that others might be set free with an inside out
experience that would eventually turn the world upside
down. An inward experience merits outward expression. An
inward relationship demands outward reflection. An inward
bond requires outward bail. One of the great contradictions
in life is that inside is always out!

On another level, you are what you eat. My mother often accused me of making a pig of myself. She was not alone.
My opponent for senior class president charged that I was

full of baloney. A classmate, upon seeing me 30 pounds heavier, exclaimed, "Holy cow!" My wife affectionately refers to me as "pickle puss" when I don't get my way, and "sweetie-pie" when she wants her way.

Health, longevity and physical make-up clearly reflect what we eat: ham and hypertension, chocolate and cholesterol, oleo and obesity. Inside is always out!

You are what you think.

Love	Lust
Liberty	License
Faith	Fear
Fullness	Failure
Peace	Peril
Prosperity	Poverty
Heaven	Hell ...

These are contradictory contemplations that lead to different destinations. The track that you are on determines your direction. Sometimes we are on the wrong track without even knowing it.

I remember the first kick ball game I ever played. The teacher picked two captains (her favorites), and they took turns choosing sides. I quickly decided which team I wanted to be on, because that captain had already gained a reputation for being the best kicker at Alexander Hamilton Elementary School. I moved close, raised my hand and yelled, "Choose me, choose me! Please, please?" I was the last to be chosen, and ended up on the other side by default. That was the first of many times I would be chosen last. I didn't understand then, but I do now. Let me explain.

I was the smallest boy in my class and have always looked 10 years younger than my age (even at age 7). Those incidents played a mind trick that was to last a very long time. If a ball came in my direction, I knew that I was going to miss it. Instead of charging aggressively, I held back and "swish," it disappeared right between my legs into centerfield. My productivity was adversely affected by my reduced expectations. Inside is always out!

I began to doubt my intelligence. When taking a test, I knew I was going to fail. Instead of studying aggressively, I held back, resorting to "wish." Why learn, when I already knew I was going to fail? Inside is always out!

I began to believe that my personality did not lend itself to popularity. When it came to girls, I was timid and shy. Instead of socializing aggressively, I held back. Why try, why wish, especially when I already knew that she would be found in the arms of another? Inside is always out!

And then something miraculous happened.

It was slow …

It was steady …

It was systematic.

The Pentecostal experience of my teenage years progressively turned me inside out. My spiritual guide took my valleys of failure and converted them into mountains of faith. He took my seeds of hatred and sowed forests of love. He took my shadows of dark despair and generated sweet sunrays of bright hope. I began to believe in myself, in my own worthiness, inside out. His confidence transformed my personal doubts into personal triumphs. Soon I was captain of my church softball team, and we won the league championship. Later I graduated with a master's degree. And when I married Doris, the woman in my life, it far exceeded my dreams.

Life is a little like computer software: garbage in, garbage out. Gospel in, gospel out. Junk imprisons us while the gospel empowers us. Lies rot; the Word of God lasts forever. Inside is always out!

Thank God, I am no longer a garbage collector.

But when they did not find them, they dragged Jason and some brethren to the rulers of the city, crying out, "These who have turned the world upside down have come here too."

—Acts 17:6

Twenty-Two

Upside Down

Ambition is a curious thing. Even with it you can fail to succeed or succeed to fail. Turn your world upside down, and you can land right side up or wrong side up. The choice is yours to make.

Lucifer was an ambitious angel. He had succeeded to number two but wanted to be number one. His cunning coup failed, and he was banished to the pit of Sheol, where he now reigns as the prince of darkness. He has been turning the world upside down and his followers have been landing wrong side up. Lucifer has …

Succeeded to fail!

God was number one but wanted to become one of us. Christ was ambitious for our souls. He suffered shame and was crucified like a common criminal upon a cross. He ascended to Heaven, where he reigns as the Prince of Peace.

He has been turning the world upside down, and his followers have been landing right side up. But in earthly terms, Christ …

Failed to succeed!

The demise of one of the world's wealthiest men of the twentieth century was a media event. For a time, he had succeeded in every secular sense of the word. Glamour, wealth and power were his, and for a time he was the envy of the world. His reign was brief, and his world was turned wrong side up. Paranoia drove him into seclusion in a sterilized suite in a Las Vegas casino. He became a recluse, a billionaire bum. He died a curiosity, his final days a pathetic sideshow. The circus continued as greed consumed those who fought over his fortune. He left nothing for good or glory. No friends mourned his passing. His life ended wrong side up. This man …

Succeeded to fail!

Another man sacrificed his career because of his devotion to others. In his job, he was promoted quickly and was headed for the top. Power and position were within his grasp. But his driving desire to be in the trenches of humanity, healing hurts, mending souls and enlarging heaven, was stronger. When he leaves this world, his probate will be minimal, but he will leave a legacy of love that will continue to multiply. In spiritual terms, this man is a zillionaire. He turned his back on the world's treasure and landed right side up. But, in earthly terms, this man clearly …

Failed to succeed!

King Saul had it all. He selfishly wanted it all for himself. His ambition took a jealous turn when he heard the women sing, "Saul has slain his thousands, and David his ten thousands" (1 Samuel 18:7b).

Jealousy and political passion consumed him. He would stop at nothing to destroy David. The end result was death by suicide. King Saul, who had it all ...

Succeeded to fail!

In one moment, Paul went from a Pharisee to a follower. In that instant, he changed from an adversary to an apostle. His faith journey led him to prison where he wrote:

> *Some indeed preach Christ even from envy and strife, and some also from goodwill: the former preach Christ from selfish ambition, not sincerely, supposing to add affliction to my chains; but the latter out of love* (Philippians 1:15-17).

> *Let nothing be done through selfish ambition or conceit, but in lowliness of mind let each esteem others better than himself. Let each of you look out not only for his own interests, but also for the interests of others. Let this [attitude] be in you which was also in Christ Jesus who ... made Himself of no reputation, taking the form of a bondservant ... humbled Himself and became obedient to the point of death, even the death of the cross. Therefore, God also has highly exalted Him and given Him the name which is above every name, that at the name of Jesus every knee should bow ... every tongue should confess that Jesus Christ is Lord, to the glory of God the Father* (Philippians 2:3-11).

For two thousand years the followers of Christ, driven

164 A Little Greatness

by love, have turned the world upside down and landed right side up. Paul, the apostolic pacesetter for the spiritual revolution, was a lowly prisoner as he, in earthly terms ...

Failed to succeed!

The magnitude of Paul's spiritual success was clearly demonstrated when he confronted the evils of the marketplace in Thessalonica. He created an uproar causing the Thessalonians to testify: "These who have turned the world upside down have come here too" (Acts 17:6).

Channel your ambition, through Christ, to the service of others, and you too can experience great joy as you fail to succeed. In the process you will turn the world ...

Upside down!

Now while Paul waited for them at Athens, his spirit was provoked within him when he saw that the city was given over to idols. Therefore he reasoned in the synagogue with the Jews and with the Gentile worshipers, and in the marketplace daily with those who happened to be there. Then certain Epicurean and Stoic philosophers encountered him. And some said, "What does this babbler want to say?"

Others said, "He seems to be a proclaimer of foreign gods," because he preached to them Jesus and the resurrection.

And they took him and brought him to the Areopagus, saying, "May we know what this new doctrine is of which you speak? For you are bringing some strange things to our ears. Therefore we want to know what these things mean." For all the Athenians and the foreigners who were there spent their time in nothing else but either to tell or to hear some new thing.

Then Paul stood and said, "Men of Athens, I perceive that in all things you are very religious; for as I was passing through and considering the objects of your worship, I even found an altar with this inscription:

TO THE UNKNOWN GOD

Therefore, the One whom you worship without knowing, Him I proclaim to you."

—*Acts 17:16-23*

Twenty-Three

Hidden in Plain Sight

The truth is often hidden in plain sight; so close, yet so very far away. It can't be found in philosophizing. It can't be discovered in debate. It can't be realized in religion. It must be mastered through a personal relationship.

The first space walk actually occurred on Mars Hill. Stoic and Epicurean philosophers walked there every day, cogitating, ruminating and speculating about the truth. You might say they were spaced out on Mars Hill. Theirs was an impersonal God, out there, somewhere.

A foreign force, a remote ruler, a distant diety.

They had even erected an altar with the inscription, *To The Unkown God.*

Paul stood in the midst of the Areopagus and said:

> *Therefore, the One whom you worship without knowing, Him I proclaim to you ... so that they should*

seek the Lord, in the hope that they might grope for
Him and find Him, though He is not far from each
one of us; for in Him we live and move and have our
being, as also some of your own poets have said, "For
we are also His offspring" (Acts 17:23a, 27-28).

Paul is saying, "The truth is right there within your grasp.
Come down to earth and enjoy a personal relationship with
your Creator."

Some elected to continue their lonely space journey
while others "joined Him and believed, among them
Dionysius the Areopagite, a woman named Damaris, and
others with them" (Acts 17:34).

Pilate looked Christ straight in the eye and said, "What
is truth?"

That's a legitimate question. We all struggle with it.

What is truth?

Another sighting of the Loch Ness monster was reported.
Intelligent people claim to have seen flying saucers. Bigfoot
has left his imprint again. As a boy, I was taken on a snipe
hunt and I did see one with my very own eyes … I did! My
son, Guy, attended a surf camp when he was younger. They
slept on the beach and were told that sand dwarfs came out
at night looking for boys who didn't stay in their tents. His
tent participated in a "lookout" vigil late into the night. My
son is now an intelligent, mature college student, and he
swears to this day that he saw sand dwarfs on the beach.

What is truth?

Modern, sincere human beings genuinely believe that
women were created to bear children and bear the burden;

that blacks have no interior and are, therefore, inferior; that the alignment of stars will align slot machine bars; that there is life after death, but it might be in the form of a sow or a cow; that voodoo determines what you do; that volcanic fire is a result of Madam Pele's ire; that crystals can cure for sure; that the Brooklyn Bridge can be bought; that you can be bought; that heaven can be bought.

What is truth?

Lenin said, "Religion is an opiate of the masses." A brilliant scholar said, "God is dead." The Beatles said, "We are more popular than Christ." A well-known religious leader said, "I am the Messiah!"

What is truth?

The Truth was standing directly in front of Pilate in plain sight, and yet he couldn't see Him. Why? Because he hadn't experienced the Truth personally. Paul was standing before King Agrippa witnessing to the power of a changed life. He concluded by saying:

> *"I am not mad ... but speak the words of truth and reason. King Agrippa, do you believe the prophets? I know that you do believe." Then Agrippa said to Paul, "You almost persuade me to become a Christian"* (Acts 26:25, 27-28).

Paul was standing directly in front of Agrippa in plain sight, witnessing to the Truth, and yet Agrippa could not see Him. Why? Because the Truth cannot be known through persuasion; He must be experienced personally.

Jesus said, "I am the way, the truth, and the life" (John 14:6a).

As a child, one of my favorite games was "hide and seek." I was a great strategist when it came to using camouflage and deception. I learned very quickly that the best hiding places were in plain sight. The person who was "it" would naturally gravitate to expected hiding areas like closets, sheds and other dark places. I would look for the obvious place and just stand there. Nine times out of ten the "it" person would walk right by me, and I would make a beeline for home base and yell, "Free!" This always worked well the first time with the new kid on the block, but it wasn't long before he was up to our tricks. When the new kid thought he knew everything, then we would resort to our real secret hiding places. Finally, he would give up and yell, "Ollie, ollie, oxen free!" And we would suddenly appear right before his very eyes. He would not learn those places until he was fully accepted as a member of the 44th Street gang.

Christ never hides. He is always in plain sight calling, "Ask, and it will be given to you; seek, and you will find; knock, and it will be opened to you" (Matthew 7:7).

With Christ you are always home free.

> *And you shall know the truth, and the truth shall make you free* (John 8:32).

Knowledge in this context requires an intimate personal relationship, one that is guaranteed to bring great joy and fellowship. He doesn't have to remain hidden.

And that's the truth!

Preaching the kingdom of God and teaching the things which concern the Lord Jesus Christ with all confidence, no one forbidding him.

—Acts 28:31

Twenty-Four

Back to the Future

As I write this final chapter, I am sitting in one of the final frontiers on earth. I am housed in a stilted thatched hut, perched on a jungle hillside overlooking a lagoon lost somewhere in the middle of the Pacific Ocean. The place is Pohnpei, an island in Micronesia, and the time is ... I'm not really sure. Intellectually, I know this is the twentieth century, but emotionally I seem to have reverted in space and time to another era. During the past nine days, I have passed through three time zones (losing a day while crossing over the date line, gaining it back on the island of Ebeye, and losing it again on Pohnpei), experienced four Sundays, and resided in three civilizations. It is a sobering thought to realize that there is an end and I must go *back to the future!*

Three questions keep arising:

Where have I been?

Where am I now?

Where will I be then?

As I write this final chapter, I am entering the final frontier of my career and calling as an active Salvation Army officer. During the past 30 years, I have passed through three decades (60s, 70s, 80s), survived four score and 40 career-threatening crises, and ministered to three distinct cultures (hippies, yippies and yuppies). They have been gratifying years, and I've even enjoyed my 15 minutes of fame. But it's a sobering thought to realize that fame is fleeting and I must return *back to the future.*

As I write this final chapter, I am entering the final frontier of my life physically, the final fourth of my four score and ten. During the past half-century, I have passed through three mid-life crises, four crash diets and survived the music of three countercultures. It's a sobering thought to realize that Elvis, Pritikin and Millie the dog have come and gone (Elvis is gone, isn't he?), and I must return *back to the future!*

Two questions remain:

What now?

What then?

When Paul was in his final chapter, he was sitting shipwrecked on an island in the middle of the Mediterranean. Undaunted, he approached the final frontier of his life and ministry. What now? What then? On this island, he confounded natives with miracles, as many were healed and converted to the cause of Christ. And from there, it was on to Rome, where Paul, even though he was to be imprisoned twice, flourished in his final years "preaching the kingdom of God and teaching the things which concern the Lord Jesus Christ with all confidence, no one forbidding him" (Acts 28:31).

It was during this time that Paul would write six of his epistles, each punctuated with spontaneous joy and permeated with the grace of God. In one of these letters, we read his final words:

> *For I am already being poured out as a drink offering, and the time of my departure is at hand. I have fought the good fight, I have finished the race, I have kept the faith. Finally, there is laid up for me the crown of righteousness, which the Lord, the righteous Judge, will give to me on that Day, and not to me only but also to all who have loved his appearing* (2 Timothy 4:6-8).

Paul knew where he had been and where he was going. He was returning *back to the future!*

It was in the final frontier of his life that John wrote the final chapter of the final book in the Book of books. This was accomplished while he was imprisoned on an island in the Aegean Sea. It was in this chapter that he recorded Christ's words:

> *Behold, I am coming quickly! Blessed is he who keeps the words of the prophecy of this book* (Revelation 22:7).

It was in this chapter that he remembered Christ's words:

> *And behold, I am coming quickly, and My reward is with Me, to give to every one according to his work* (Revelation 22:12).

It was in this chapter that he recalled Christ's words:

*I am Alpha and Omega, the Beginning and the End,
the First and the Last ... the Bright and Morning
Star* (Revelation 22:13, 16b).

Wow! Christ knows where He's been, where He is now, and where He is going. I never quite thought of it in this particular context before, but He is the eternal past, present and *future!*

That means that the final frontier is not so final after all. That means that my failures can be forgotten. That means that my life and ministry are just beginning to flourish. That means that there is another island to reach and another book to be written. That's what the poet meant when she wrote ...

*When we have exhausted our store of endurance,
When our strength has failed 'ere the day is half done,
When we reach the end of our hoarded resources
Our Father's full giving is only begun.
His love has no limits, his grace has no measure,
His power no boundary known unto men;
For out of his infinite riches in Jesus
He giveth, and giveth, and giveth again.*

Annie Johnson Flint (1866-1932)

With Christ the end is always the beginning, the Bright and Morning Star. Incredible as it may seem, to go back to the future is to go ...

FORWARD TO THE BEGINNING!

Forward!

Since there is no such thing as an ending in the Christian life, it seems logical and proper to place the "forward" here. The message of this book does not end. It has been written to give you encouragement. True saints do not waver from their purpose. They never accept the status quo. They always march forward. Such forward progress is called "glory."

There is glory in God, in Christ and in Christians, and the glory is Christ in them, and this is *in turn* ... the hope of glory (Colossians 1:27).

> *Now the Lord is the Spirit, and where the Spirit of the Lord is, there is freedom. And we all with unveiled face, beholding the glory of the Lord, are being changed into His likeness from one degree of glory to another; for this comes from the Lord who is the Spirit* (2 Corinthians 3:17-18, RSV).

For the Apostle Paul, glory is a partially fulfilled reality, although it is a future expectation, into which we enter by degrees. In this little book, greatness and glory are synonymous. I have already experienced a little greatness (glory) in this life. I have led a child to Christ who is now grown and leading other children to Christ. I have led a homemaker to Christ who is now leading other women to Christ. I have led a retiree to Christ who now, 10 years later, is still leading other retirees to Christ. I've seen thousands moved and motivated by our programs and productions. I am not the same person I was 20 years ago, nor two days ago, and I'm still moving forward.

Are you 20, 40 or 80 years of age? Keep moving forward, because greatness still resides within you, and ultimate glory is yours to share. We may never meet face to face in this life. But I do want to say "aloha" and wish you *a little greatness!*

When we meet in heaven, I'll give you a great big bear hug. Just look for the short, shaveless, shining saint with the great big smile, shouting ...

Great Glory!

Something to Think About

◄○►

Bible Study and Discussion Guide

This *Bible Study and Discussion Guide* is designed to be used by the reader independently or as part of a study group.

It provides a 26-week framework (24 chapters plus prologue and forward) for home Bible study. Participants should read chapter and Scripture portions in advance. The Bible study facilitator will prepare questions and comments to enhance discussion and participation.

This guide can also be used individually to enhance daily devotions. It is suggested that each chapter be re-read on consecutive days and an alternating question considered each day. The prayer subject should be personalized daily. Repetition is crucial to an effective devotional and prayer regimen.

Prologue

1. Read the Beatitudes (Matthew 5:1-12) and discuss the eight contrasts on greatness as compared to world standards.

- If you are blessed in this spiritual sense, when should you rejoice and be exceedingly glad?

2. Read how Jesus fulfills the Law (Matthew 5:17-19; 7:12) and discuss the meaning of greatness in this context.

- How can we fulfill the Law today?

3. Read John 14:16 and discuss who "another Helper" is.

- From personal experience, make a list of helps available to you today.

4. Read Acts 1:18; 4:33 and Ephesians 1:17-23. Discuss the phrase, "exceeding greatness of His power" (Ephesians 1:19) in the context of these passages.

- Is this power available today? Share some examples of that power.

5. Pause and pray to be filled with the fullness of His power.

One

1. Read Genesis 1:1-2 and Acts 2:1-13. Discuss how God always brings order out of chaos.

   • Give some biblical and historical examples.

   • Give some personal examples.

2. Re-read "The Great Musical Revival" and discuss which instrument in the orchestra fits your personality.

   • Now "blow your own horn" for a moment, and share your gifts and talents with the group.

3. Read Romans 12:1-16 and discuss how your differences and individuality can blend together for the common good of the whole.

   • Why do we need each other, and how does our Christian fellowship give us greater power?

4. Discuss the potential for harmony in every discordant life in the context of the five following statements:

- Sickness can lead to submission.

- Failure can lead to success.

- Loss can lead to serenity.

- Calvary can lead to salvation.

- Pentecost can lead to surrender.

5. Pause and pray for personal and collective harmony.

Two

1. Discuss the proliferation of revenge themes found in the media today.

   • Share some of your own past and present feelings of personal revenge.

2. Read Romans 12:17-21 and discuss the phrase, "Vengeance is Mine, I will repay ..."

   • What did the writer of Proverbs mean when he said, "Heap coals of fire on his head"?

3. Read John 8:1-11, and discuss the concept of love in this context.

   • Can you honestly share some of the "stone throwing" episodes in your life?

4. Read Acts 4:1-12 and discuss the power of unconditional love. Why is this an attribute of greatness?

   • Share some examples of the healing power of love.

5. Pause and pray for someone who has hurt you. Place that person on your "coals of fire" list and think of a specific way to overcome evil with good.

Three

1. Read Matthew 14:28-33 and John 18:1-18. Consider the boldness of Peter prior to Pentecost.

   • Share some examples of pre-Pentecostal boldness (personal and non-personal) practiced today.

2. Read Acts 4:1-22 and consider the boldness of Peter after Pentecost.

   • How did Pentecost re-define the meaning of boldness?

   • How did those in authority respond to this new gentle boldness? Why?

   • How did the people respond? Why?

3. Re-read Acts 4:7, 8, 13 and discuss the power behind this new-found boldness.

• What part does education and training play?

4. Read Acts 4:23-31 and discuss the importance of prayer in this process.

5. Pause and personalize the Apostles' prayer for boldness.

Four

1. Read John 14:1-21 and discuss why Christ had to leave.

   • Why was the void between the Ascension and Pentecost important for His followers?

   • Can that same void exist within His followers today?

   • How does it manifest itself?

2. Read Luke 21:1-4 and discuss why the widow was considered great in God's eyes.

   • What was the difference between the rich giver and the poor widow?

   • How do these differences apply to holy living?

3. Read Matthew 10:37-42 and discuss how much the Christian is expected to give.

4. Read Acts 4:2-37 and apply these principles to present-day practices.

• What role should the church play in meeting needs?

• What is your responsibility?

5. Pause and pray that the Holy Spirit will fill the void with a giving heart.

• Pray specifically for those you know in need. Do something about it.

Five

1. Read Jonah 2:1-10 and discuss the positives that resulted from Jonah's negative experience.

• Why are negative experiences sometimes necessary?

• Share some personal experiences and results.

2. Read Mark 15:24-41 and discuss why Calvary was necessary.

• Why must we "take up our cross," and what does that mean?

• Share some personal Calvary experiences.

3. Read John 21:18-23 and discuss, in this context, how the Calvary experience may differ with each follower.

• Discuss some specific present-day differences.

4. Read Acts 2:7 and 12-14. Consider the progress made since Calvary.

• Why were the Apostles held in high esteem? Would they always be held in this high regard?

• Discuss the difference between self-esteem and spiritual esteem.

5. Pause and pray for the Spirit to fill you with His esteem and power.

Six

1. Read Acts 5:15-16 and discuss the spiritual significance of the shadow.

   • Share some personal experiences where someone's shadow has fallen on you.

2. Read Mark 8:22-26 and discuss the significance of Christ's second touch.

   • Share some touching experiences in your life.

3. Read Isaiah 49:2 and discuss the Messiah's mission in the context of this prophecy.

4. Read Acts 2:3-4 and discuss the significance of being filled with the Holy Spirit in light of the above prophecy.

   • How can we reflect that mission in our life and ministry today?

5. Pause and pray that your spiritual shadow will brighten the soul and ignite the spirit of another.

   • Thank God for the spiritual shadows that have touched your life.

Seven

1. Read Acts 5:28-39 and discuss the phrase, "We ought to obey God rather than men."

   • What was the significance of Gamaliel's advice?

   • How can we apply that advice to our life and ministry?

2. Read Matthew 22:17-21 and consider the extent of our obedience in this context.

3. Read Mark 7:1-23 and discuss traditions, compromises and contradictions that may exist in the Church today.

   • Share some personal compromises that you have made.

4. Re-read Acts 5:39 and consider why obedience to God rather than men can bring great power.

5. Pause and pledge anew your obedience to God. Pray for a clean heart.

Eight

1. Read Acts 5:40-42 and discuss why you think the apostles counted it worthy to suffer shame.

  • How does the phrase, "… for His name," clarify the meaning of this attitude?

2. Read Hebrews 12:1-3 and discuss why the phrase "scorning its shame" has eternal significance.

3. Read Matthew 10:38 and discuss why the cross is a symbol of true greatness and power.

  • Share the reaction of family, associates and others to the sacrifice you have made (positives and negatives).

4. Read Luke 15:11-24 and discuss the concept of worthiness in this context.

  • Share some of the reasons you count it worthy to suffer shame for His name.

5. Pause and "fix [your] eyes on Jesus, the Author and Perfecter of our faith."

  • Thank Him for enduring the cross and scorning its shame. Pray for those who think it's a shame.

Nine

1. Read Ephesians 2:4-10 and discuss the spontaneous nature of God's grace.

• Share some examples of how that grace has been duplicated in your Christian living.

2. Read Acts 6:1-6 and discuss the qualifications for servanthood.

• Share those avenues of service in which you are now engaged.

3. Read Matthew 20:17-28. Discuss ambition in this context.

• What do you think motivated the mother of James and John?

4. Re-read Matthew 20:26-28, and discuss the meaning of greatness revealed there.

  • What sacrifices are required for this kind of greatness?

  • What sacrifices are you making?

5. Pause and pray for the gift of grace. Pray for opportunities for service.

Ten

1. Read Acts 6:7-8 and discuss the phrase "full of faith and power, did great wonders and signs …"

• What do you think some of those wonders and signs were?

• Do we have wonders and signs today?

2. Re-read Ephesians 2:8 and discuss why faith and grace are so closely linked together.

• How are they connected?

3. Read Luke 17:5-6 and consider what Jesus had to say about faith in this context.

4. Read Matthew 17:19-21 and discuss how much faith is needed for a miracle.

• How are prayers and faith linked?

5. Pause and pray for enlightenment and power to use the faith that you already have. Consider specific prayer requests.

Eleven

1. Read John 14:1-31 and discuss the questions asked by Thomas, Philip and Judas. How do these questions reflect their faith?

 • Discuss some of the questions you may have today.

2. Read John 14:12 and discuss the phrase "greater works."

 • What are the implications for ministry today?

3. Read John 14:11-15 and consider the four components of His "greater works" formula.

 • How does He help us in this process?

4. Read Luke 11:5-13 and consider the fifth component to this formula.

 • Share together some examples of answered prayer.

5. Pause and thank Him for answered prayer. Consider prayer requests.

Twelve

1. Read Acts 6:9-15 and discuss the accuracy of the accusations made against Stephen.

   • Have similar accusations ever been made against you? Share them with the group.

2. Read Acts 7:1-53 and discuss Stephen's response to their accusations. Consider his emotional state as he responded.

   • Was his response based on innuendo and hearsay?

   • How have you responded in similar circumstances?

3. Read Acts 7:54-60 and Luke 23:32-43. Compare the two portions of Scripture.

   • What is the lesson for us today?

4. Read Romans 3:23 and 1 John 1:9. Discuss how we can walk that delicate line that separates the sin from the sinner.

5. Pause and pray for forgiveness. Ask the Lord to forgive those who have sinned against you.

Thirteen

1. Read Acts 8:1-17 and discuss why Simon the sorcerer was considered great.

   • How did Simon respond to Philip?

   • Consider the term "greatness" as applied to Simon and Philip.

2. Read Matthew 27:15-25 and compare the greatness of Pilate with the greatness of Christ.

   • Draw some comparisons from your present-day experiences.

3. Re-read Mark 8:22-26 and discuss the concepts of spiritual blindness and spiritual sight implied.

4. Read John 20:1-10 and consider the implications of the resurrection.

• Why does Christianity differ from other religions?

• Share some of the reasons why you, personally, are different from the non-Christian.

5. Pause and pray for spiritual sight and insight. Pray for friends and family who are spiritually blind.

Fourteen

1. Read Acts 8:15-17 and discuss how Simon and the others could be baptized without receiving the Holy Spirit.

2. Read Acts 8:18-22 and discuss baptism of the Holy Spirit as the gift of God or work of grace.

- Discuss the extent and availability of God's grace.

- Share some examples of how His grace has manifested itself in your life over a period of time.

3. Discuss the following components of grace:

- It can't be taught.

- It can't be bought.

- It can't be sought.

4. Read Matthew 11:11-15 and discuss "He who has ears to hear, let him hear!" in the context of grace and its availability.

• Also consider the phrase "He who is least in the kingdom of Heaven is greater than he" in this same framework.

5. Pause and praise Him for His manifold grace. Ask Him to fill you afresh with His peace, power and presence.

Fifteen

1. Read Acts 8:23-25 and discuss the phrase "poisoned by bitterness" in this context.

  • Share some bitter moments in your life.

  • Write an ending to Simon the sorcerer's story and share it with the group.

2. Read John 21:25 and discuss what this fact has to do with our faith.

3. Read Psalm 45:1 and Hebrew 4:16. Discuss the difference between a bitter experience and a bittersweet experience.

  • How does God help us cope with our present troubles?

4. Read Romans 5:3-8 and 1 Peter 1:3-4. Discuss why we should glory in tribulations.

  • What is our hope in this life?

5. Pause and pray about any remaining bitterness in your heart. Give thanks to God for the hope that we find in His resurrection.

Sixteen

1. Read the following Scripture portions and discuss the contagious grace reflected in each story:

A. John 2:1-11

B. John 9:1-41

C. Luke 17:11-19

D. Acts 8:26-40

E. Acts 9:36-42

• Share personal examples of this contagious grace.

2. Pause and pray for others who you want to receive this grace and joy. Thank God that your name is written in the heavenly headlines.

Seventeen

1. Read Psalm 23 and discuss the phrase "My cup runs over" as it relates to great joy.

   • Finish the phrase "My cup runs over because …"

2. Read Philippians 4 and discuss how Paul could write these words of joy while he was in prison.

3. Read Matthew 26:26-29 and discuss how Jesus could give thanks when He knew what lay before Him.

   • What did He mean when He said, "Drink from it, all of you?"

   • Share personal examples of overflowing joy, even during the most difficult of times.

4. Read Acts 9:1-19 and discuss why it was important for Paul to be blinded so that he might see.

5. Read Acts 9:23-35 and consider the change in Paul's life.

   • Discuss whether real joy comes from within or without.

6. Pause and pray that your cup will be filled with joy even in times of difficulty.

   • Pray that your sight will be raised and you will be used to raise the sights of others.

Eighteen

1. Read John 4 and discuss why it was a problem for Jesus to be speaking to a Samaritan, to a woman, to a woman of questionable character.

   • Discuss parallels today or in this century.

2. Read Acts 10:9-22 and Leviticus 2. Discuss the dilemma Peter was facing.

   • Consider the phrase, "God has made clean" in this context.

3. Read Acts 10:23-35 and consider how God's revelation relates to Cornelius.

   • Relate the phrase, "In truth I perceived that God shows no partiality," to this century. Does this problem still exist today?

4. Read Acts 10:36 and discuss the phrase, "He is Lord of all," in this context.

   • Share the differences that may exist within your study group.

5. Pause and ask God to reveal your partialities and forgive your differences. Pray for peace.

Nineteen

1. Read Acts 11:1-3 and discuss the brethren's criticism of Peter's newly inspired direction.

• Discuss some of the criticisms of others that exist in your fellowship. Are these criticisms justified?

2. Read Acts 11:15-17 and discuss the phrase, "God gave them the same gift as He gave us …"

• What effect does this statement have on the "criticisms" you have just discussed?

3. Read Acts 11:18 and consider why "repentance to life" is a "far out" experience.

• Use the term "omnipresent" in expressing God's relationship to you personally.

4. Read 1 Peter 1:8 and Acts 11:19-26. Describe how the Christian can find unity in diversity.

• What does the title "Christian" signify today? What responsibility does the title bring today?

5. Pause and pray for the Holy Spirit to find His way in so that you can find your way out. Pray for unity.

Twenty

1. Read the accompanying Scripture and discuss the following statements in light of this chapter.

"We are born with our limitations."
• Are limitations barriers?

"We are bound by our ability."
Exodus 18:18; 19; 21; Matthew 28:18; John 14:27; Acts 13:29
• Why do we need others?

"We are loosed by our vision."
• Share some dramatic turning points in your life.

"We are stretched by our determination."
• Complete the following sentence: "I have been stretched through ..."

"We are empowered by His presence."
John 14:2-3

2. Pause and pray to be empowered by His presence. Thank God for His promise to prepare a place for you.

Twenty-One

1. Read Acts 12:6-17. Discuss how Peter turned a negative experience inside to a positive one outside.

- How was he assisted?

- How did he respond?

- How did the others respond?

2. What is meant by, "one of the great contradictions in life is that inside is always out?"

3. Make a list of those influences (angels) who have helped to lead you out of a bondage experience. Share one "inside out" experience with the group.

4. Consider the two following tracks:

love	lust
liberty	license
faith	fear
fullness	failure
peace	peril
prosperity	poverty
heaven	hell

• How does what we think determine the track we are on?

• What must we do to get on the right track?

• How does the "Pentecostal experience" help us to stay on the right track?

• What is expected of us?

5. Pause and praise Him for placing you on the right track. Pray for strength to share your "inside out" experience with others. Go and share.

Twenty-Two

1. What is meant when we say that Lucifer succeeded to fail and Christ failed to succeed. Discuss the contrast between the two.

2. Read 1 Samuel 18 and discuss why King Saul's success led to failure. How does this contrast with David's life experience?

3. Share with the group some present day examples of failing to succeed and succeeding to fail. You may want to personalize these examples by sharing your own testimony.

4. Read Philippians 1:15-17 and 2:3-11. List the appropriate words and phrases from these Scripture references under the following headings:

Ambition   **Attitude**

5. Read Acts 17:1-6 and discuss how the Church used these attitudes to turn the world upside down.

6. Pause and pray, "Let these attitudes be in me (us) which were also in Christ Jesus who made Himself of no reputation, taking the form of a servant, humbling Himself and became obedient to the point of death, even the death of the cross."

7. Sing or recite together in unison the following:
   He is Lord, He is Lord,
   He is risen from the dead and He is Lord.
   Every knee shall bow, every tongue confess
   That Jesus Christ is Lord.

Twenty-Three

1. Read Acts 17:16-34 and discuss the dilemma the philosophers were facing.

   • What kind of God were they worshiping?

   • Where was their God?

   • What was their relationship to the God they worshiped?

   • How did they worship Him?

2. Discuss and answer the following questions:

   • What is truth?

   • How can we know the truth?

3. Share with each other your personal relationship with the Creator.

4. Discuss how the truth has made you free.

5. Pause and enjoy a personal relationship with the Creator. Thank Him for the freedom He has given you. Agree together upon a petition you would corporately make to the Lord. Now ask freely.

Twenty-Four

1. Read Acts 28 and discuss Paul's ministry in the final years of his life. How does this speak to your life and future?

2. Read 2 Timothy 4:6-8. Write one defining paragraph and one personal illustration under the following phrases:

• Fought the Good Fight

• Kept the Faith

• Finished the Race

• Crown of Righteousness

(You have just written the outline for a sermon)

3. Read Revelation 22 and discuss your future in the light of these promises.

4. Answer the following questions:

- Where have I been?

- Where am I now?

- Where will I be then?

5. Pause and praise Him by singing or reciting the following:

When we have exhausted our store of endurance
When our strength has failed 'ere the day is half done,
When we reach the end of our hoarded resources
Our Father's full giving is only begun.

His love has no limit, his grace has no measure,
His power no boundary known unto men;
For out of his infinite riches in Jesus
He giveth, and giveth, and giveth again.

6. Thank Him for His "full giving" and pray for a new beginning.

Forward

1. Read Colossians 1:27 and discuss the hope of glory and what it means as you move forward.

2. Read 2 Corinthians 3:17-18. Consider the phrase, "being changed into His likeness from one degree of glory to another." Share some recent changes that have taken place in your life. Take a moment and write down changes you would still like to make.

3. Discuss how greatness and glory are synonymous. Share some of your "glory" experiences.

4. Complete the phrase, "I'm still moving toward …"

5. Pause and pray for a vision of His present and future glory. Give praise by singing or reciting the following:

Lo! a new creation dawning!
   Lo! I rise to life divine!
In my soul an Easter morning;
   I am Christ's and Christ is mine.

Glory, Glory, Jesus saves me
   Glory, Glory to the Lamb!
O the cleansing blood has reached me
   Glory, Glory to the Lamb!
                    (Attr. Francis Bottome 1823-94)

Let the journey forward begin!